fruit and vegetable
carving

fruit and vegetable
carving

FOOD CRAFT AT YOUR FINGERTIPS

Marie Elsa Lobo

© Brijbasi Art Press Ltd.
A-81, Sector V, Noida-201301
Uttar Pradesh, India

First published by Brijbasi Art Press Ltd. 2006

Text: Marie Elsa Lobo

Photography: Karan Khanna

Design: Yogesh Suraksha Design Studio
www.ysdesignstudio.com

Edited by: Nasima Aziz

Project Coordinator: Veena Baswani

ISBN 81-87902-26-4

Processed, printed and bound at

Brijbasi Art Press Ltd.
E-46/11, Okhla Industrial Area, Phase-II
New Delhi-110020, India

c   o   n   t

To my husband Jimmy

The presentation of food, artistically garnished, has always fascinated me. There was never an occasion when my guests failed to be impressed with my ideas for transforming a plain table into something unusual and exciting.

When I first heard about vegetable carving, a traditional Siamese Palace Art, I had no inkling of the role it was going to play in my life. I was a busy housewife, devoted to my husband, Jimmy, who was a doctor with the Indian Army. We had an exceptionally busy social life, our house always crowded with family and friends, and we needed no excuse to throw a party. I enjoyed entertaining, and my special signature was the experimental style with which the food was garnished.

One day all this changed: my husband suddenly died.

As I struggled to recover from my loss I tried to divert my mind with vegetable carving. I had no training in this art. My teacher was a road-side vegetable vendor in Crawford Market in Mumbai. I watched, squatting down at street level, as he transformed red radishes into roses. Handing me my first carving tool, a piece of a razor blade attached with wire to a wooden stick, he taught me how to apply the correct pressure, the way to rhythmically turn the vegetable, to reveal the rose that lay within the radish, to find serenity in the ordinary things of life.

My second carving tool was devised by the knife grinder, trundling his cycle around my neighbourhood: he shaped the handle of a teaspoon into the working end, with the bowl providing the grip.

What started as a therapy for adjusting to a new way of life turned into a profession.

After many years of experience in this field, conducting innumerable demonstrations and teaching classes both in India and abroad, I feel confident in sharing my art with you through this book.

The simple instructions given for each garnish need to be followed with care and patience. Very soon you will find yourself becoming creative and daring, experimenting with your own techniques and developing your own garnishes.

You may begin to look around you and find a world of beauty and inspiration hidden in the things around you, waiting to be discovered.

While there is nothing quite like the excitement of getting an idea, giving that idea form and substance can sometimes be a long and tedious task. However, the writing of this book was nothing but a pleasure because of the support and encouragement of my family and friends. The enthusiasm they displayed in the project helped me to carry out this dream.

Verna, Tony, Aruna, and Rohini, I thank you for your constant love and unwavering confidence in my ability to achieve. My nieces kept assuring me that I was the best.

My loving thanks to Tara and Bina my steadfast companions who, with their creative input and dedication, have contributed to this venture.

Were it not for friends like Tessa Menezes and Sheila Bajaj, who found time to encourage and support my efforts with exceptional warmth, the idea for this book may perhaps have been stillborn. I thank them most affectionately.

For those of you who feel you are all thumbs — there is hope! Start with the right tools and you are halfway to success.

1. **A CARVING KNIFE OR A PARING KNIFE**
   This knife should have a short flexible blade and a short handle, comfortable to hold and easy to control. In fact it should be an extention of your hand.

2. **A VEGETABLE PEELER**
   An indispensable tool for cleaning and paring vegetables.

3. **A PAIR OF SCISSORS**
   This is used to trim away excess material, cut out leaf shapes, etc.

4. **A VEGETABLE SLICER**
   A gadget to facilitate slicing vegetables thinly and evenly.

2

5. **DECORATOR TOOLS**
   These are specialised tools which have different types of blades. The V-shaped blade and the scallop blade are invaluable for cutting decorative edges and for carving various flowers. They give the finished product a professional look.

6. **THE SPIRAL SLICER**
   This tool will transform your vegetables into decorative spiral streamers.

7. **FIXERS**
   Bamboo skewers in various sizes, toothpicks, pins and rubber bands. A small hammer to push the skewer into hard surfaces.

8. **MISCELLANEOUS**
   Small bottles of food colour; small bowls to dilute the colour; paintbrush; felt pens; large flat plastic boxes for soaking the garnishes in iced water and also for storing the garnishes in the refrigerator.

With a little imagination petals can be cut from tomatoes, pumpkins, carrots, cucumbers, and brinjals (aubergines). There are a variety of leaves and herbs that can be used to enhance your creation: parsley, mint, dill as well as red and green cabbage leaves. Try using small cutters to stamp out different shapes for flower petals. For example, cut thin ovals of tomato and smaller diamond shapes of brinjal (aubergine). Place the diamonds on the ovals to create an exotic flower. Or you can cut petal shapes from pumpkin and make the flower centre with beetroot (Fig. 1).

3

Trim off both ends of a carrot (Fig. 2). Score the outside with a corrugated garnishing tool (Fig. 3). Use a knife to slice flowers of the desired thickness (Fig. 4). Fit a round piece of beetroot in the centre.

Cucumber spirals can make a meat platter look exotic. Choose small tender cucumbers that have few seeds and use the spiral slicer.

Bite-sized sandwiches can be made in different shapes with the aid of cutters (Fig. 5). Treat your guests to a creatively arranged sandwich board of cold cuts and breads and you will hold the winning hand at your next card party.

- THE GARNISH YOU CHOOSE SHOULD COMPLIMENT THE FOOD IT IS PLACED WITH. IT SHOULD NEVER MASK OR OVERPOWER THE FLAVOUR OF THE FOOD, EVEN IF THE GARNISH IS FOR DISPLAY ONLY.

- SELECT FRUITS AND VEGETABLES THAT ARE WITHOUT BLEMISHES OR BRUISES.

- ALL VEGETABLES SHOULD BE WASHED AND DRIED BEFORE USE. THEY SHOULD NEVER BE FROZEN.

- TAKE YOUR TIME, FOLLOW INSTRUCTIONS CLOSELY AND WORK SLOWLY AND GENTLY.

- ALL GARNISHES MUST BE IMMERSED IN A BOWL OF ICED WATER IN WHICH ICE CUBES HAVE BEEN ADDED SO THAT IT REMAINS COLD LONGER. THE VEGETABLES BECOME CRISP AND LOOK THEIR BEST. IT HELPS VEGETABLES SUCH AS ONIONS AND CARROTS TO 'BLOOM'. AFTER SOAKING FOR ABOUT AN HOUR DRAIN THE GARNISHES AND STORE THEM IN AN AIRTIGHT BOX IN THE REFRIGERATOR. THEY CAN BE PREPARED IN ADVANCE AND STORED READY FOR USE.

- FOOD COLOURS GIVE A NEW DIMENSION TO THE GARNISHES. TAKE A BOWL OF CHILLED WATER AND ADD A FEW DROPS OF THE DESIRED COLOUR. AFTER THE 'BLOOMING' PROCESS IS COMPLETE, DIP THE GARNISH IN THE COLOURED WATER FOR A FEW MINUTES; REMOVE AND DRAIN. ONIONS AND RADISHES ABSORB COLOUR WELL. YOU MAY ALSO APPLY MORE CONCENTRATED COLOUR WITH A PAINTBRUSH.

- ANY FIRM FRUIT OR VEGETABLE CAN BE USED AS A BASE FOR AN ARRANGEMENT. YAM (*SURAN*) IS EXTREMELY VERSATILE. FOR EXAMPLE, HUMPTY DUMPTY'S WALL IS MADE OF YAM.

l e t's

h a v e a

party

CHESSBOARD SANDWICHES

For the dark squares:
• **8** SLICES BROWN BREAD • **2** CUCUMBERS • **2** TSP SALT
• **30-60** G BUTTER, SOFTENED • BLACK PEPPER TO TASTE

1. Thinly slice the cucumbers, arrange the slices in a
   layer on a plate, sprinkle with the salt and leave for
   30 minutes to extract some of the liquid. Rinse off
   the salt under cold running water; pat dry.
2. Butter each slice of bread, arrange the cucumber
   on four slices, seasoning with pepper and additional
   salt if required. Cover with the remaining slices to
   make four sandwiches. Remove the crusts and cut
   each sandwich into four squares.

For the light squares:
• **8** SLICES WHITE BREAD • **30** G BUTTER, SOFTENED
• **I** TBSP MAYONNAISE • **2** EGGS, HARD-BOILED,
CHOPPED • **I** CAN TUNA FISH • SALT AND PEPPER TO TASTE

1. In a bowl mix the butter, mayonnaise, eggs, tuna, salt
   and pepper. Spread evenly on the bread slices and
   make four sandwiches. Remove the crusts and cut
   each sandwich into four squares.
2. Arrange the 16 small sandwiches on a flat platter,
   alternating the brown and the white, to create a
   chessboard effect. Make figures seated on either
   side of the chessboard (see Dwarf p. 113).

CARD DELIGHT SANDWICHES

Note: You will require small cutters in the shape of hearts, diamonds, spades and clubs.

- 8 SLICES BROWN BREAD • 8 SLICES WHITE BREAD
- 6 TBSP BUTTER, SOFTENED • ½ TSP MUSTARD PASTE
- ½ TSP DILL, (*SOYA KA SAAG*), CHOPPED • SALT AND PEPPER TO TASTE • 8 SLICES ANY COLD CUTS (THINLY SLICED HAM, ROAST BEEF, ROAST CHICKEN ETC.)
- 8 SLICES CHEESE
- 3 SMALL POTATOES, PARBOILED, PEELED

1. Mix half the butter with mustard, salt and pepper and spread it on the brown bread.
2. Mix the rest of the butter with dill, salt and pepper, and spread it on the white bread.
3. Make sandwiches using three slices of bread, alternating the colours, (buttered sides towards the middle), with the cold cuts between one layer and the cheese between the second layer.
4. Using the cutters, cut into shapes. If desired, pierce a toothpick through each sandwich with an olive at the end of the toothpick.
5. For the dice: Cut each potato into a cube, using a sharp knife. Pierce each side of the cube with peppercorns in an arrangement to resemble dice.

RAINBOW LAYERED PANCAKE

For the pancake batter:
- 1 CUP FLOUR   1 EGG • ¼ CUP MILK • WATER AS REQUIRED
- SALT TO TASTE

For the fillings:
3 TYPES OF FILLING IN DIFFERENT COLOURS, GIVEN BELOW

1. Whisk the egg in a bowl; add flour, milk and a little water and beat until the batter is smooth.
2. Heat a small frying pan; grease it lightly and pour in just enough batter, about 2 tablespoons. Tilt the pan so that the batter is evenly distributed. When it leaves the sides flip out the pancake.
3. Repeat this process until all the batter is used up and a stack of pancakes is ready.
4. Place one pancake on a flat dish and spread the spinach filling over it. Place another pancake to sandwich the first and spread the tomato paste over it. Place a third pancake over the second one, and cover with the cheese filling. Repeat the layers to make a rainbow cake; decorate the top with semi-circles of tomato.
5. Garnish the platter with chopped lettuce and any vegetable flower such as a carrot Peony (see p. 44).

For the spinach filling:
- 2 SMALL BUNCHES SPINACH, WASHED, CHOPPED
- 1 TBSP OIL • 1 ONION, DICED • 2 GREEN CHILLIES, SLICED
- SALT AND PEPPER TO TASTE   ½ TSP SUGAR

Heat the oil in a pan and fry the onion, then add the spinach, green chillies, salt, pepper and sugar. Cook till limp; cool, then purée in a blender.

For the tomato paste:
- 4 LARGE TOMATOES, SKINNED, CHOPPED • 1 TBSP OIL
- 1 ONION, CHOPPED • ¼ TSP RED CHILLI POWDER
- ¼ TSP SAFFRON • SALT AND PEPPER TO TASTE • 1 EGG

Heat the oil in a pan, fry the onion, then add the tomatoes, red chilli powder, saffron, salt and pepper. Cook till soft; add the egg and stir vigorously.

For the cheese filling:
1 TBSP BUTTER • 1 TSP FLOUR • ⅓ CUP MILK • ½ CUP CREAM CHEESE • ¼ CUP CHEESE, GRATED • 2 TBSP MAYONNAISE
- 1 CAPSICUM, FINELY MINCED • SALT AND PEPPER TO TASTE

Heat the butter in a pan, add the flour and stir for a minute; add the milk and mix till smooth. Remove from the stove and add the cream cheese, cheese, mayonnaise, capsicum, salt and pepper.

FISH MOULDED SALAD

1 CAN TUNA FISH, FLAKED • 3 TBSP MAYONNAISE • 2 EGGS, HARD-BOILED, CHOPPED • 2 CAPSICUMS, MINCED • 1 ONION, MINCED
1 POTATO, BOILED • 1 TBSP LEMON JUICE

1. In a bowl, mix all the ingredients together. Pile the mixture into a flat dish and shape it with your hands to resemble a fish. Spread some more mayonnaise on the top.
2. Use semi-circular slices of red radish to represent scales, and slivers of carrot to outline the head, mouth and tail. Place a slice of stuffed olive for the eye. Decorate the platter with shredded lettuce and onion flowers.

MEAT LOAF

- 500 G BEEF, MINCED • 500 G PORK, MINCED • 1 PACKET BACON
- 1 TSP LEMON JUICE • A FEW PEPPERCORNS • SALT TO TASTE • 4–5 SLICES BREAD • 3 EGGS • 1 EGG, HARD-BOILED

1. Pressure cook the beef, pork, bacon, lemon juice and peppercorns together. Take out some of the stock, soak 4–5 slices of bread in it and add them to the mince. Dry up the rest of the liquid on high heat; cool, purée in a blender, adding a little more lemon juice and salt if required. Add the eggs.
2. Put this mixture into a meat loaf mould and steam for 20 minutes.
3. Chill the meat loaf then un-mould it onto a flat platter. Insert slivers of red radish in the front of the loaf to resemble a brick wall. Make a small Humpty Dumpty (see p. 108) using a hard-boiled egg and make him sit on the wall. Paint a face on the egg with felt pens. Decorate the platter with shredded lettuce and any vegetable flower such as a turnip Daisy (see p. 64).

CRISPY SHRIMP

- 20 LARGE PRAWNS, SHELLED, DE-VEINED (LEAVE THE TAIL SHELL ON)
- 1½ TSP SALT   1½ TBSP WHITE WINE

For the batter:
- 1 EGG, BEATEN • 3 TBSP FLOUR • ¼ TSP SALT • ⅓ TSP BAKING POWDER

OIL for frying

For the Sweet and Sour Sauce:
- 1 TBSP OIL • 1 TSP GARLIC, MINCED • 1 TBSP SOYA SAUCE • 3 TBSP SUGAR
- 2 TBSP VINEGAR • 4 TBSP KETCHUP • 1 CUP OF WATER
- 1 TBSP CORNFLOUR, DISSOLVED IN ¼ CUP WATER

1. Rub the prawns with 1 tsp of the salt; wash and drain. Sprinkle the prawns with the wine and the rest of the salt and set aside.
2. Mix the egg, flour, salt and baking powder and make a batter.
3. Heat the oil in a wok. Dip the prawns in the batter and deep-fry them until they become light brown. Remove with a slotted spoon; drain. Serve on a bed of lettuce.
4. Heat 1 tbsp oil, fry the garlic, add the soya sauce, sugar, vinegar, ketchup and water. Bring to a boil, stir in the cornflour and simmer the sauce until it thickens.
5. Fill a Cucumber Boat (see p. 72) with sauce and arrange the shrimp around it.

PORCUPINES

- 2 GRAPEFRUIT OR ORANGES
- 150 G CHEESE, CUBED
- 1 SMALL CAN PINEAPPLE BITS
- 20 COCKTAIL SAUSAGES
- 4 STUFFED OLIVES
- 2 GHERKINS
- 50 COCKTAIL STICKS

1. Cut off a slice from the grapefruit/orange to create a firm base. With a toothpick pierce holes and
   insert half an olive for each of the eyes and a gherkin for the nose, using pins or slivers of toothpick
   as required. Repeat the same with the second grapefruit/orange.

2. Pierce the cheese and pineapple bits on cocktail sticks and fix them all over one of the porcupines.
   Put the sausages on cocktail sticks and fix them on the other porcupine.

PINWHEEL SANDWICHES

- I LOAF OF WHITE OR BROWN BREAD, (NOT SLICED)
- 3 TYPES OF SANDWICH FILLINGS, IN THREE COLOURS
- SOME CELERY AND CARROT, CUT INTO STICKS
- SOME CHERRY TOMATOES

Egg Filling:
- 60 G BUTTER, SOFTENED • 2 EGGS, HARD-BOILED
- I LEVEL TBSP MAYONNAISE • SALT AND PEPPER TO TASTE

Chicken Filling:
- 100 G CREAM CHEESE • 2 TBSP YOGHURT • I TBSP CHICKEN
SOUP POWDER • ½ CUP COOKED CHICKEN, FINELY CHOPPED
- I TSP CELERY, FINELY SLICED • SALT AND PEPPER TO TASTE

Tomato Filling:
- 100 G CREAM CHEESE • 2 TBSP YOGHURT • I TBSP TOMATO
SOUP • ½ TSP CHILLI POWDER • I CAPSICUM, FINELY DICED
- SALT TO TASTE

1. Slice the loaf of bread horizontally as thin as possible. Remove the crusts from all the sides. Lightly flatten each long rectangle of bread with a rolling pin.
2. Cut the celery and carrot sticks to fit the short side of the rectangle.
3. Blend the fillings in separate bowls.
4. Cover each of the bread rectangles with a different filling. Place the carrot or celery across one end then roll up tightly, pressing the edge down firmly. Wrap each roll in cling film or foil and chill until required. (For smaller sandwiches cut the long rectangle into half).
5. Slice the rolls to make pinwheels having different fillings and colours.
6. Make the Peacock (see p. 52) and place it at the edge of a round platter. Arrange the pinwheel sandwiches in a circle around the peacock to resemble peacock feathers open in a fan. Arrange small red cherry tomatoes between the sandwiches and garnish the platter with cabbage leaves.

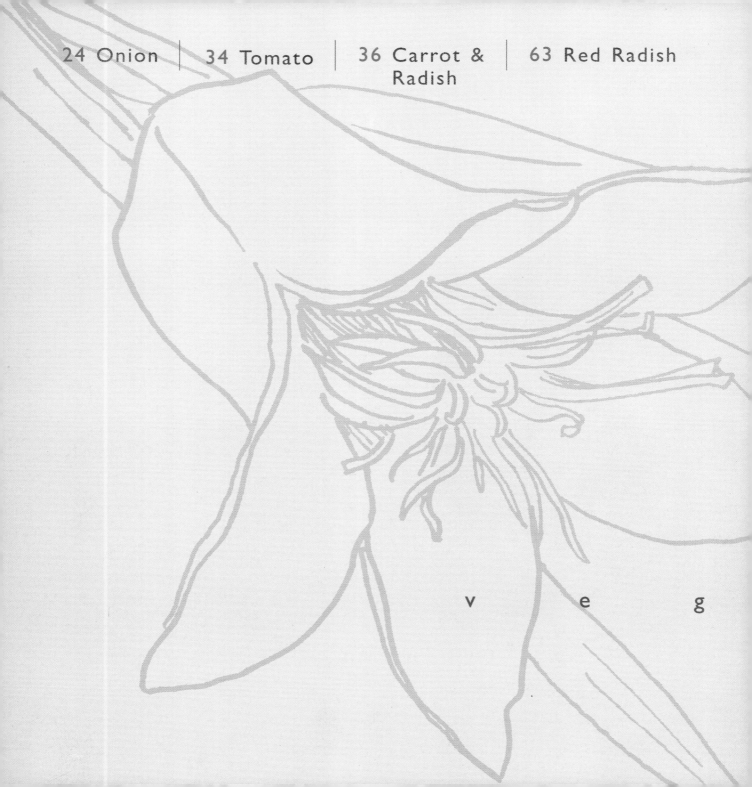

v e g

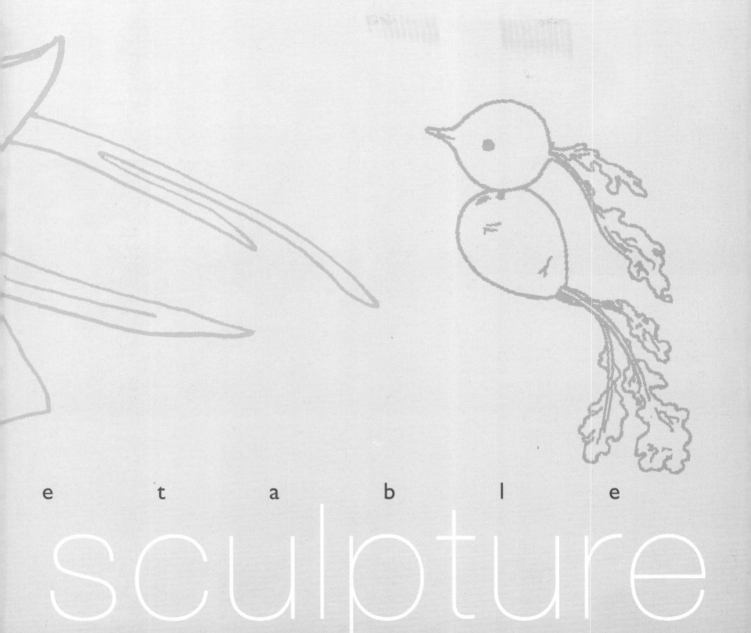

e t a b l e

sculpture

L I L Y

Cut off a 5 cm (2") piece of spring onion to make the flower.

Starting 1 cm (½") away from the root pierce downwards with a sharp knife slitting all the way through to the centre of the bulb and stalk. Continue to make deep vertical slits all around the bulb.

Separate these straight petals and immerse in iced water for half an hour to allow the lily to open out and bloom. Drain; dip into the colour of your choice if desired.

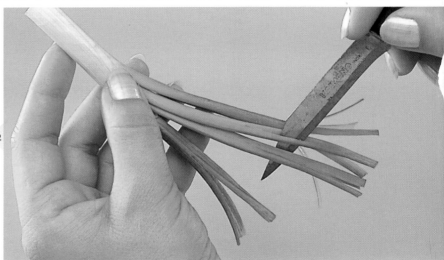

For the leaves, cut the green stem tubes at different levels. Turn the stalk upside down and shred about 5 cm (2") of the tubes into strips.

Immerse in iced water so that the ends curl. (Note: The green fronds so formed can be used in many vegetable creations.)

Pierce a skewer into the base of the flower; insert the other end of the skewer into one of the tubes of spring onion greens and push it in till the stick is hidden.

• 1 LARGE ONION • YELLOW FOOD COLOUR • TOOTHPICKS
• SOME CABBAGE LEAVES (DARK, OUTER LEAVES)

CHRYSANTHEMUM

1

Remove the dry outer skin of the onion. Cut off 1 cm (½")
from the top, stem end.

Make as many thin, vertical cuts as possible from the top to the
bottom, stopping 60 mm (¼") away from the root end. The cuts should
penetrate to the centre of the onion.

2

Gently open out the petals.
Immerse the onion in iced water for
10 minutes; drain. Mix ¼ tsp yellow food colour in a bowl of
iced water and immerse the flower for 2 minutes; drain.

3

Shake the flower gently
to dry it and open out its petals.

Cut the cabbage leaf to resemble a chrysanthemum leaf.

4

T U B E R O S E

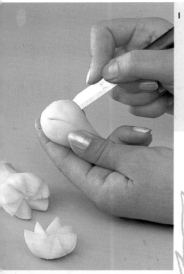

1

Cut the onion bulbs to a length of about 6-7.5 cm (2½-3").

Hold the root end up and make deep zigzag cuts into the bulb, through all the layers to the centre. Separate the long and the short flower and use the short flower elsewhere.

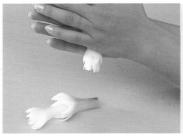

2

Gently roll the long flower between the palms to loosen the layers, then carefully pull out each hollow-tube flower.

4

Carefully pull a flap with your finger and insert the hollow tube of a flower. Note that pulling the flap too hard will break it.

Fix several flowers to the drumstick, using the smaller ones on top and the larger ones as you go lower.

3

Keep the drumstick upright and cut off the top. Make cuts 3.8 cm (1½") apart.

5

Fix the smallest flower with a toothpick right on top of the drumstick.

To form the leaves slit the tubes of broad onion greens through one side, open out and flatten.

Cut with scissors into leaf shapes. Curl each leaf with the blade of the scissors.

6

7

Use pins to attach one set of leaves to either side of the drumstick

SAY IT WITH FLOWERS
A striking arrangement of tuberoses, crysanthemuns
and roses made from onions

L O T U S

Remove the dry outer layers of the onion.

Keeping the root end of the onion at the bottom, cut 5 to 7 triangular, lotus-shaped petals, using just enough pressure to cut one layer of onion.

Cut off the tip and gently separate the petals.

Similarly, cut 2 or 3 more layers so that the centre of the petals of the next row falls between the petals of the previous one. Take care to go through only one layer at a time. Open out the petals of the lotus each time.

Cut the remaining onion bulb flat across the middle.

Soak the lotus in iced water for 30 minutes; drain. Using a paint brush, apply yellow food colour to the centre of the flower and put splashes of red colour on the petals.

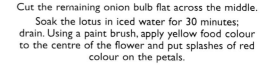

Make either heart-shaped or circular leaves out of watermelon rind.

• 1 LARGE, BULBOUS WHITE ONION • FOOD COLOUR

ROSE

1

Remove the dry outer skin of the onion.

Starting slightly above the bottom, make 4 or 5 scallops around the onion, going through 2 layers only.

Discard the part above the scallops in those 2 layers.

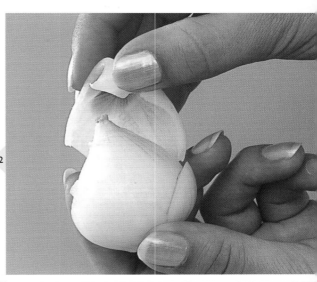

2

3

Repeat the steps, alternating the petal positions.

4

5

Immerse the rose in iced water for at least half an hour; drain. Mix ¼ tsp any food colour of your choice in a bowl of iced water and immerse the flower for 2 minutes; drain. Insert a toothpick under the flower.

As the centre is reached it is not possible to make more petals. Make 3 deep cuts to form a triangle and remove it, leaving a bud shape in the centre of the rose.

SERENITY
Graceful swans glide amid
lotus and lily blooms — all made of onions

• 3 OR 4 LARGE, LONG ONIONS, WHITE OR RED, FOR THE FEATHERS • A PIECE OF RADISH 10 CM (4") LONG AND
ABOUT 2.5 CM (1") IN DIAMETER, FOR THE BODY • 1 SLENDER, CURVED SPRING ONION, FOR THE NECK
• A SLICE OF CARROT 60 MM (¼") THICK, FOR THE BEAK • PEPPERCORNS FOR THE EYES • PINS

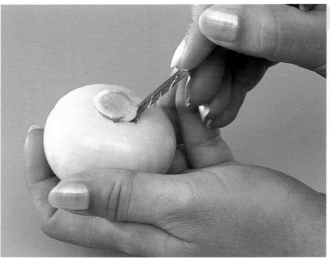

To make the feathers, scoop out the root end of the onion. Make sure the inside is not a double onion.

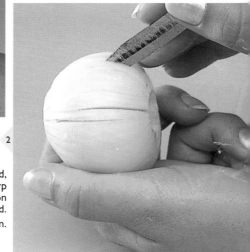

Starting 1 cm (½") away from the stem end, make deep, close, vertical cuts with a sharp knife, right through to the centre of the onion and down through the scooped root end.
Make cuts all round the onion.

Now release each layer carefully and lay the layers out according to size.

For the last cut, slit the onion right to the centre. This will separate the layers.

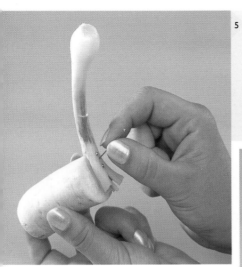

5

Shape the radish piece to taper towards one end.

On the opposite side attach the stem of the spring onion with 3 or 4 long pins. The bulb of the spring onion forms the head of the swan.

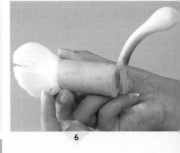

6

7

Starting with the smallest, attach the feathers to the tapered end, using pins on either side.

To create a water-filled pond: Cook china grass (available at Indian groceries) according to the instructions on the packet, add blue food colour, pour into a shallow dish and place in the refrigerator until set. Cut blocks of yam to form the sides of the pond.

Continue attaching layers of feathers so that they overlap You will require 5 to 6 feather layers to cover the swan's body up to the neck. Attach one more feather to cover the front fora nice finish.

8

From a flat piece of carrot carve out a u-shaped beak and attach it to a toothpick, partly slitting the front of the beak to open it.

Pierce a hole in the head and insert the beak. Pierce holes on either side of the head and insert peppercorn eyes.

Note: Your swan's character depends on the shape of the spring onion bulb/head and the curve of stem/neck.

• 1 LARGE, VERY FIRM TOMATO, EITHER GREEN OR RED FOR THE BODY
• 1 SLENDER, CURVED SPRING ONION FOR THE HEAD AND NECK • A PIECE OF CARROT FOR THE BEAK
• CLOVES OR PEPPERCORNS FOR THE EYES • TOOTHPICKS • PINS

1 From the top of the tomato carve out a tiny oval-shaped wedge and reserve. Cut out 3 more ovals parallel to the first. Remove and reserve.

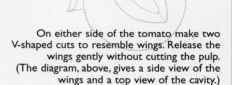

2 On either side of the tomato make two V-shaped cuts to resemble wings. Release the wings gently without cutting the pulp. (The diagram, above, gives a side view of the wings and a top view of the cavity.)

3 Insert the ovals in their original order inside the cavity, staggering them by about 1 cm (½"), and tilting them upwards. Pierce a toothpick through all but the smallest wedge to keep them in place.
Insert the smallest wedge on top.

Cut a thin slice from the side of the tomato to rest the tomato on this stable base.

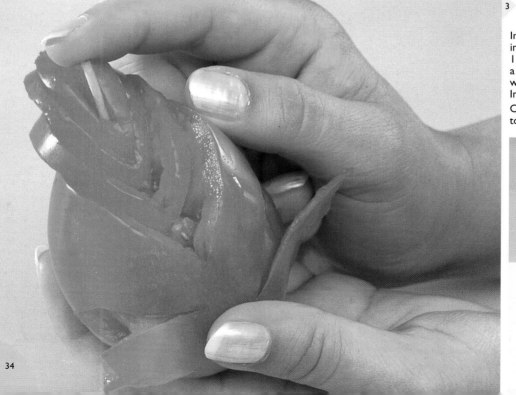

4 Fix a triangular carrot beak to the root end of the spring onion, using a toothpick. Make small holes on either side of the head and insert peppercorn eyes.

Place the onion neck in the small gap in the cavity in front of the wedges and attach it with a toothpick.

WAR AND PEACE
A hot discussion between two birds,
Mr. Green and Mr. Red, made from tomatoes

CANDLE

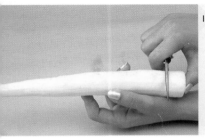

I

Use a peeler to make the carrot/ radish perfectly smooth and even in shape.
Starting from the broad end, mark about 2.5 cm (1") for the decorated base.

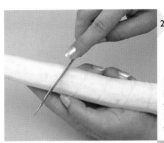

2

Make a spiral incision with a knife all around the vegetable to the tip. Hold the knife at an angle in one hand and roll the vegetable in the other hand.

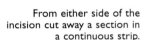

3

From either side of the incision cut away a section in a continuous strip.

4

Round off the edges of the incision to make them deep and smooth.

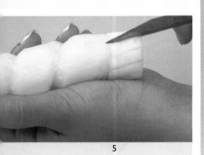

5

For the decorated base make parallel vertical wedge-shaped grooves.

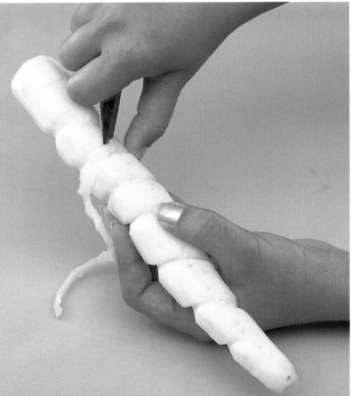

6

Make a cavity at the tip of the candle and insert a wick coated with wax, or a small birthday candle. Or shape a candle flame out of a piece of carrot and attach it with a toothpick. Immerse the candle in iced water for about an hour; drain.

Colour a radish candle by dipping it in coloured water if you want.

C A N D L E   S T A N D

Cut a 10 cm (4") block from the carrot.
At a height of 1" from the narrow end make a
1 cm (½") deep cut all around the carrot block.

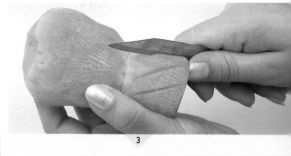

2

Scrape away the carrot from above
the cut to form a base and reveal
a wine glass shape.

Make the carrot surface smooth
and rounded, using a peeler.
Cut a 2.5 cm (1") circle in the middle
of the top surface and scoop it to
make a hole.

3

To decorate the base: Cut vertical or diagonal
grooves to make a pattern. Deepen the groove
with one straight cut and the next at a slant to
achieve depth, discarding the cut-out strip.

4

Leaving a plain area around the hole, mark one
row of evenly-spaced triangles. Deepen the lines
to make a clear design.

Continue making evenly spaced diamonds till the
bottom of the cone.

Immerse the candle stand in iced water for about
an hour. Remove and drain. Pierce a strong wooden
skewer of the required length into the centre of
the hole and insert a candle in the stand.

Note: If green pumpkin is used, the natural shape
is maintained and only the design is carved out.

ANNIVERSARY SPECIAL
A day to remember!
The lit candles in their candle stands
made from radishes and carrots will leave
romantic memories

• 1 LARGE, TAPERED CARROT • SOME SPRING ONION GREENS
• 1 BAMBOO SKEWER

GINGER FLOWER

1

About 2.5 cm (1") below the stem end of the carrot make a circular cut and shape it into a cylinder to form the stem of the flower.

Shape the part just below this stem so that it slopes down gently.

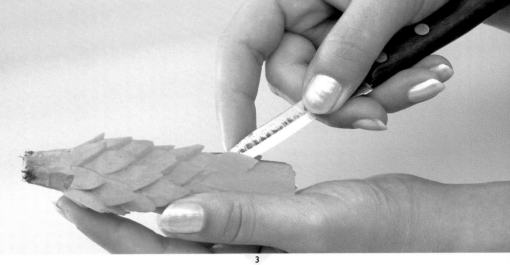

3

In the next row carve the petals of the flower, positioning them alternately with the first row. Repeat the steps and continue to make petals, tapering downwards to the tip of the carrot.

Make diamond-shaped grooves in each petal of the flower but not in the calyx.

4

2

On this sloping surface pierce about eight V-shaped, shallow petals for the calyx, cutting away from under the tip of the petals to partially release them.

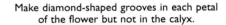

5

Immerse the completed ginger flower
in iced water for at least an hour.

Pierce a skewer into the base of the flower;
insert the other end of the skewer into
one of the tubes of spring onion greens
and push it in till the stick is hidden.

LOLLIPOP FLOWER

Slice off a small segment from the tip of the carrot and carve the broad end into a cone.

Insert a sharp knife into the carrot at a slight angle and with a circular movement carve five petals. The curve of the petal should extend to the edge of the cone.

Cut away a circular section from under the petals so as to expose them.

In the same manner carve out a second row of petals, positioning them so that they come in between those in the first row.

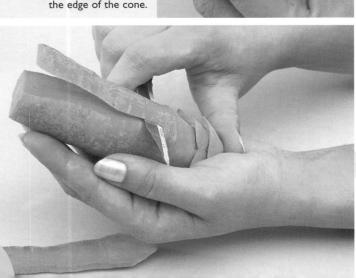

Below this cut off a slice from either side of the carrot.

On both the broader sides make wedge-shaped cuts down the whole length of the carrot. Accentuate the curve of each wedge and make it smooth.

6

From the side without wedges cut thin slices, stopping just above the petal shapes. Space the slices so that you get five segments in all.

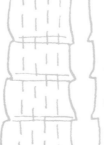

7

Immerse the lollipop flower in iced water to bloom; drain. Pierce a skewer into the base of the flower; insert the other end of the skewer into one of the tubes of spring onion greens and push it in till the stick is hidden.

43

• I FAT, CYLINDRICAL CARROT OR RADISH
• SOME SPRING ONION GREENS • I BAMBOO SKEWER

I

Cut a 7.5 cm (3")
segment from the broad
end of a carrot.

2

Curve both ends of the block
using a peeler.

3

Cut out and discard small sections
of carrot to leave a wedge-shaped design
around the curved ends.

The curved top slopes
down on both sides.

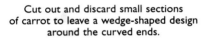

4

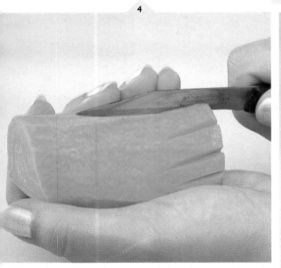

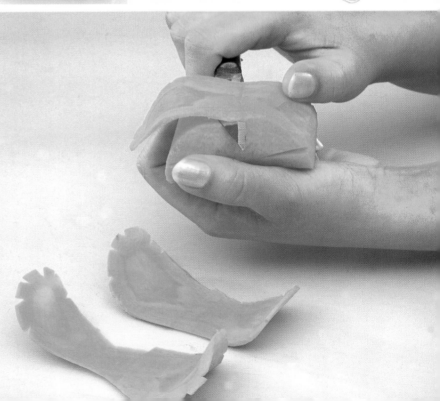

5

Holding the block to keep it steady,
carefully cut thin slices along the curved
side to make about 6 petals.

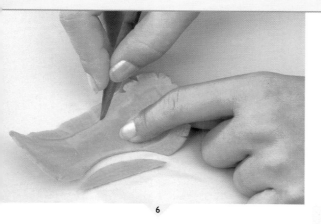

7

From the remaining carrot cut a rectangular piece for the stopper and pierce it on to a skewer.

8

Pierce the petals on the skewer, starting with the largest petal. Alternate the position of the petals so that they are at right angles to each other. End with the smallest petal.

6

Carve each petal to resemble a figure 8 by narrowing the middle portion.

9

Cut a thick slice of carrot for the centre and make a criss-cross design on one side. Attach the carrot centre to the tip of the skewer to complete the flower.

10

Immerse the peony in iced water for at least an hour to allow it to bloom.
Insert the other end of the skewer into one of the tubes of spring onion greens and push it in till the stick is hidden.

- I CARROT OR RADISH, ABOUT 20 CM (8") LONG
- I BAMBOO SKEWER

SPIDER CHRYSANTHEMUM

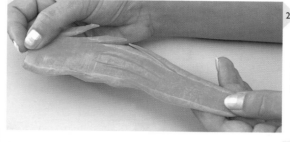

Position two cuts on the broad end and one cut on the narrow end, on both sides of each petal. Then cut two parallel grooves in the centre. (See diagram.)

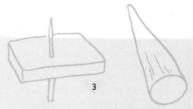

With the remaining vegetable, cut a rectangle about 5 cm (2") long for the stopper. Also carve a long cone for the centre.

Peel the carrot.
Using a slicer, cut about 6 long slices which taper from the broad end to the narrow end. Or use a knife to cut extremely thin slices.
Trim each slice in the shape of a petal.

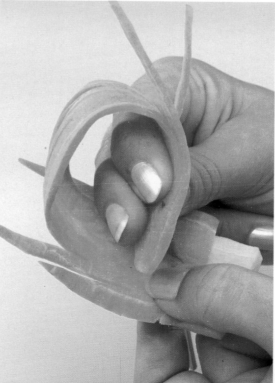

Insert a skewer through the stopper then pierce it through the broad end of the first petal. Bring the other end towards the skewer and, twisting it slightly, fix it on the skewer.

Continue in the same manner to arrange the other petals.
Insert the long cone into the tip of the skewer to hold the petals in place.
Immerse in iced water for one hour; drain.

• I FAT RADISH • I STRAIGHT THICK SPRING ONION BULB FOR THE CENTRE
• SOME SPRING ONION GREENS FOR STEM AND LEAVES • BAMBOO SKEWER, TOOTHPICKS, PINS

E A S T E R   L I L Y

1

Cut a 12 cm (5") section from the broad end of the radish.

Mark 5 equal parts on the cross section and cut 5 panels along the side of the radish so that it forms a column that tapers downwards.

Slice each panel from the top till halfway down the block to make petals.

With the tip of a knife cut away the inner portion of the column, working along the base of each petal.

2

Discard the inner column.

Turn the flower upside down and place it on a board. Cut and shape the petals.

Immerse the flower in iced water. After an hour or two, when it has 'bloomed', paint pink streaks on the base of the petals.

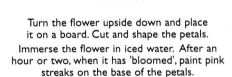

3

4

Hold the spring onion bulb with the root end up and starting
1 cm (½") away from the root pierce downwards with a sharp knife
slitting all the way through to the centre of the bulb and stalk.
Continue to make deep vertical slits around the bulb. Separate
these straight petals and immerse in iced water for half an hour
to allow the lily to open out and bloom. Colour it yellow.

5

To form the leaves slit the tubes of broad onion
greens through one side, open out and flatten.
Cut with scissors into leaf shapes.
Curl each leaf with the blade of the scissors.

6

Attach the yellow onion lily inside the Easter lily with a toothpick.
Pierce a skewer into the base of the flower; insert the other end of
the skewer into one of the tubes of spring onion greens and push it in
till the stick is hidden. Attach the leaves on either side with pins.

SYMPHONY IN WHITE
An elegant arrangement
for Easter — lilies made
from radishes

50

PEACOCK

I

Cut the broad end of a carrot into a cone.
Pare the cone with a sharp knife to get two flat rings.
Give the outer edges of the rings a zigzag design to
create collar feathers.

2

Slice the carrots
lengthways, using a slicer,
to get about 25 slices.

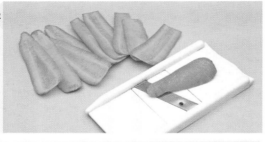

Cut a 10 cm (4") section from the radish.
Trim the curved spring onion to an appropriate
size. Attach the spring onion head to one end of
the radish body using a toothpick.

Make small scalloped slits along the body,
alternating the positions. There should be
at least 3 slits in a row.

4

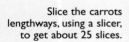

3

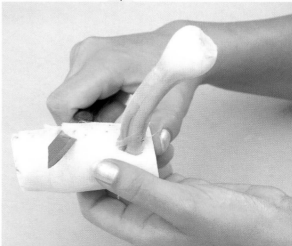

Round off the broad end and straighten the narrow end of each slice;
cut out v-shaped sections along the edge to resemble feathers.
Select 3 different lengths for the feathers.

5

Starting from the end opposite the head, fix carrot feathers into the slits with pins, using the longest feathers first.

6

Continue up the body to the head, ending with the shortest feathers.

7

Set the collar feathers at the base of the neck, fixing them with pins.

Cut a triangular beak from the carrot and a serrated crest from a slice of beetroot.

8

Pierce holes on either side of the head and insert the peppercorn eyes. Attach the beak with a sliver of toothpick.

Attach the crest to the top of the head with a pin.

Mount the peacock on a block of yam or melon so that the tail feathers cascade over the side.

- 1 FAT RADISH • A PIECE OF CARROT FOR THE BEAK AND THE FEET
- PEPPERCORNS FOR THE EYES • TOOTHPICKS • PINS

S W A N

1

Cut a block about 15-18 cm (6-7")
long from the radish.
Cut two slices lengthways from either
side of this block to be used for wings.

2

Cut out wing shapes, placing
one over the other to
achieve symmetry.
Feather the edges by cutting
out 5 or 6 wedge-shaped
triangles on the longer side
of each wing.

3

Make a V-shaped cut in the
radish at one-third distance
from one end.
Shape the neck from the
shorter section and the body
from the longer section.

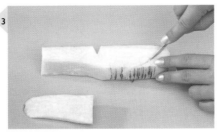

4

Use a peeler to round off the contours of the bird's body. Make
two slits on either side of the body for inserting the wings.

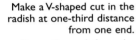

5

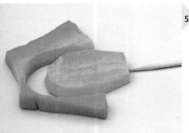

From a flat piece of carrot carve out
a u-shaped beak and attach it to a
toothpick, partly slitting the front of the
beak to open it.

6

From 2 slices of carrot cut out the webbed feet.

7

Insert the wings into the side slits and fix them with toothpicks.
Make two cuts under the body, insert the feet and fix them with
pins. Scoop out a hole at the end of the neck and insert the beak
into the hole. Make small holes and insert peppercorns eyes on
either side of the head.

A PAIR OF SWANS
These elegant white swans made from radishes
alight on a marshy island

• I FAT CARROT
• PEPPERCORNS FOR THE EYES • TOOTHPICKS • PINS

Cut off a 7.5 cm (3") section
from the broad end of
the carrot.

Using a peeler, shape the section
into a cone, making sure that the
broad end is well rounded.

Keep the broad end facing you
and holding the knife at right
angles to the surface, cut out a
cone-shaped hole in the centre,
about I cm (½") wide.

Use the knife to mark
a circle around the hole.

Scoop out the carrot between
the hole and the circle, so that it
forms a round, protruding mouth.

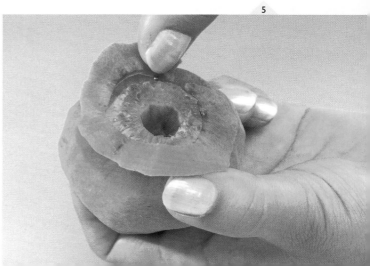

Cut a curved slice near the
broad end to stand the goldfish
on its side

7

Above the mouth carve 2 semicircles to form eyeballs and scoop out the surrounding carrot so that the eyeballs stand out.

8

Cut out fine, parallel grooves, about 60 mm (¼") apart, running from the head to the tail of the fish. Make more grooves at right angles to form a criss-cross pattern.

Cut out an L-shaped section 1 cm (½") high and 60 mm (¼") deep at the tail end.

9

Slice 3 thin pieces for the tail from the remaining carrot, by hand or with a slicer. Shape and fashion the edges. For the fins, cut a 5 x 1 cm (2" x ½") rectangle of carrot into half, lengthways, and make zigzag cuts on both halves.

Fan the tail fronds and fix them with a toothpick inside the L-shaped section. Make small holes and insert the peppercorn eyes.

10

Make deep slits on either side of the body, insert the fins and fix them with pins.

Immerse the goldfish in iced water for an hour.

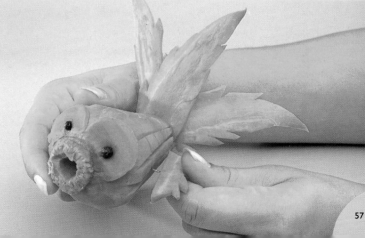

LOVEBIRD

I

Scrape the radish then cut off and discard 2 slices lengthways to get 2 flat surfaces.

Cut two thin slices lengthways from either side for the wings.

2

Carve out a wing, place it on the second slice to achieve uniformity and carve the second wing.

Feather each wing by cutting wedge-shaped segments along the lower curve.

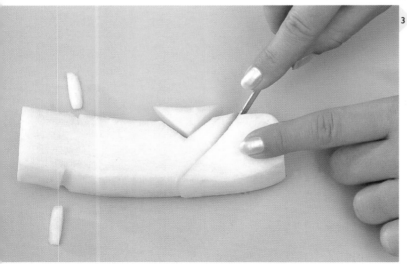

3 Shape the radish into a block. About a quarter of the distance from one end of the block make 2 notches where the neck will come. About a third of the distance from the other end make a deep V-shaped cut where the tail will start. Cut diagonally across the block to create the tail.

Use a peeler to round off the contours of the bird's head and body, trimming away any sharp edges. Shape a long, conical beak out of the carrot piece and insert a toothpick into it.

4

Scoop a hole in the front of the head and insert the beak. Make two slits on either side for fitting the wings and attach the wings with toothpicks. Make small holes and insert the peppercorn eyes on either side of the head.

• I FAT CARROT • PEPPERCORNS FOR THE EYES
• TOOTHPICKS • PINS

P I G

Cut off a section of carrot from the broad end, 10-12 cm (4-5") long.

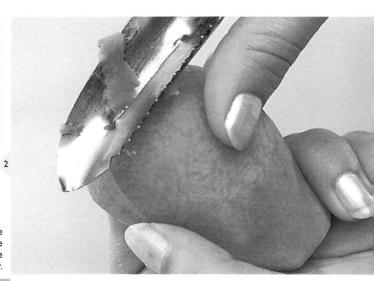

One-third of this block is the face of the pig and two-thirds is the body. Shape the face on the narrow end and round off the broad end with a peeler.

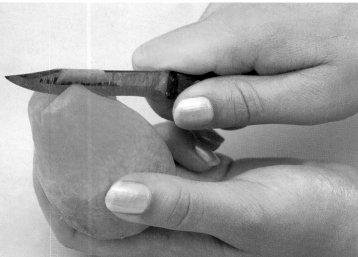

(a) On the face cut and discard a 60 mm (¼") deep triangle for the mouth.
Make two slits for inserting the ears.

(b) Cut a slice of carrot about 1 cm (½") in diameter. Cut off a quarter of it and discard, and use the remaining portion as the snout.

(c) From another slice of carrot cut out two leaf-shaped ears, about 1" long.

(d) From yet another slice of carrot cut a thin, circular tail.

(e) Take a cylindrical block of carrot about 2.5 cm (1") high and cut it vertically into 4 equal parts for the legs. Cut and curve one side of the leg to fit against the pig's round body. To shape the hoof, cut away a triangular notch in the middle of the foot.

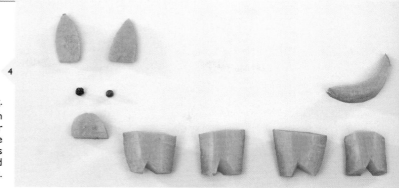

Assemble all the parts of the pig.
Fix the snout to the upper part of the mouth with two pins as nostrils. Make shallow grooves and fit 2 legs on either side of the body with pins or toothpicks. Insert the ears into the prepared slits and fix with pins. Position the peppercorn eyes between the ears. Make a triangular groove on the pig's rear and put the tail into the groove, fixing it with a pin.

- I FAT CARROT, RADISH OR YAM
- PEPPERCORNS OR MUSTARD SEEDS FOR THE EYES

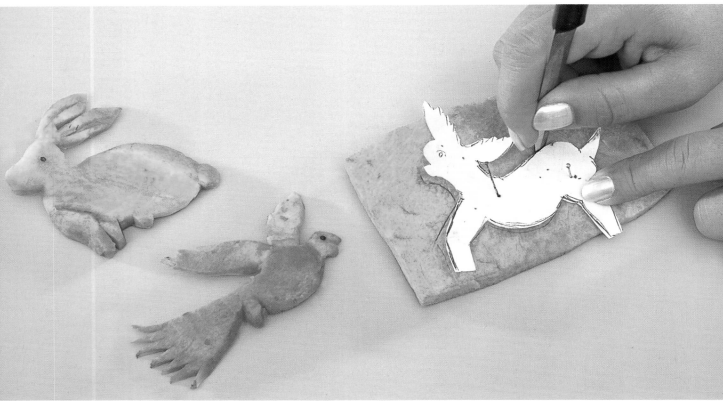

Make a regular, straight-sided block out of any of the above vegetables. It should be about I cm (½") thick. Make a paper pattern to the shape of any animal or bird you wish to cut.

Place the pattern on the surface of the block. Hold the knife perpendicular and pierce slowly along the edge of the pattern to avoid the under section getting mutilated. If the block is large enough place more than one pattern at a time.

Trim the edges of the cut-out, rounding off wherever required. Slice into two cross sections to make duplicates. Make small holes and insert peppercorn or mustard seed eyes. Immerse in iced water.

• 1 SMALL, ROUND RED RADISH FOR THE HEAD **• 1** SLIGHTLY LARGER RED RADISH FOR THE BODY **•** SPRIGS OF PARSLEY, AS REQUIRED **• 2** CLOVES **•** TOOTHPICKS

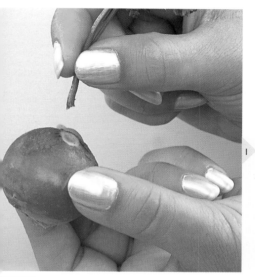

1 Retain the root of the small red radish, trimming it to resemble a beak. Retain some of the small fresh leaves and trim them to resemble a crest.

In case there are no leaves on the small red radish, make a hole and insert a sprig of parsley for the crest.

Cut off the root of the large radish but retain the leaves to resemble tail feathers, or attach a sprig of parsley with a pin.

2

Fix the small red radish on top of the large red radish with a toothpick.

Insert cloves for the eyes.

DAISY

1

Shape the top of the turnip into a cone.

2

Flatten the top of the cone, then use a scallop tool to carve petals all around the outer surface. Cut deep, inserting the tool at the broad end of the cone and pushing towards its narrow end.

3

When the last petal is cut, the flower will detach. Immerse the flower in iced water for an hour. To make another flower, scrape the corrugated surface of the cone to make it smooth and repeat the process.

4

Cut a thick slice of carrot for the centre and make a criss-cross design on one side.

5

Pierce a skewer through the base of the flower and into the carrot centre.

6

Insert the other end of the skewer into one of the tubes of spring onion greens and push it in till the stick is hidden.

FLOWER FIESTA
The vibrant freshness of daffodils and daisies,
made from carrots and turnips, enliven a tea party

• I LARGE TURNIP • I MEDIUM CARROT
• SOME SPRING ONION GREENS • I BAMBOO SKEWER

DAFFODIL

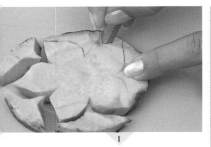

2

Carve out two thin wedge-shaped slits in the centre of each petal.

I

Cut a 60 mm (¼") thick round
slice from the turnip.
Carve five equal petals on the slice.

Reduce the thickness of each petal from the underside
so that the edges are thin.

3

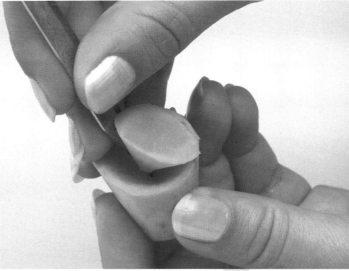

4

Cut a cylindrical block of carrot about
2.5 cm (1") high and shape it like a tumbler.
Cut out a deep cone from inside
the tumbler, leaving a thin wall.

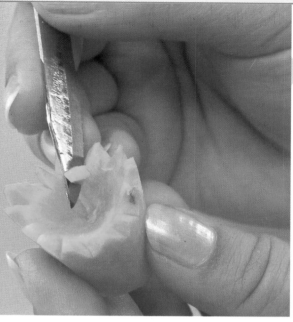

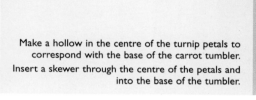

Cut fine zigzag notches along the circumference of the tumbler.

Make a hollow in the centre of the turnip petals to correspond with the base of the carrot tumbler.

Insert a skewer through the centre of the petals and into the base of the tumbler.

To form the leaves slit the tubes of broad onion greens through one side, open out and flatten.

Cut with scissors into leaf shapes.

Insert the other end of the skewer into one of the tubes of spring onion greens and push it in till the stick is hidden.

Attach the leaves on either side with pins.

CUCUMBER

DUCK

• I CURVED CUCUMBER, BROAD AT ONE END, FOR THE BODY
• I STRAIGHT CUCUMBER OF THE SAME COLOUR FOR THE WINGS
• A PIECE OF CARROT FOR THE BEAK AND FEET • PEPPERCORNS FOR THE EYES • TOOTHPICKS • PINS

2

Feather the edges by cutting out 5 or 6 wedge-shaped triangles on the longer side of each wing.

I

From the straight cucumber cut two long slices from either side for the wings.

3

From the remaining portion of the straight cucumber cut out a rectangular piece then shape it to form the tail feather, carving deep zigzags on the top.

4

From 2 slices of carrot
cut out the webbed feet.

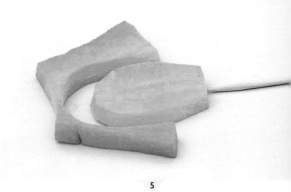

5

From a flat piece of carrot carve out
a u-shaped beak and attach it to a toothpick,
partly slitting the front of the beak to open it.

6

Under the broad end of the curved cucumber cut a thin slice to stabilise the duck,
making sure that the cucumber, the body of the duck, curves upwards.
At the narrow stem end mark a square for attaching the beak,
then deepen it into a hole.
At the opposite broad end, remove an L-shaped section for inserting the tail feather.
Make two curved slits on either side of the body for attaching the wings.

7

Insert the wings into the slits and fix them with pins or toothpicks.
Insert the beak into the square hole prepared on the head.
Fix the tail feather into the L-shaped slit at the opposite end.
Make two cuts on the underside, insert the webbed feet and secure with pins.
Make small holes and insert the peppercorn eyes on either side of the head.

ENCOUNTER
Ducks and goldfish, made from
cucumbers and carrots, come out to play

• I STRAIGHT CUCUMBER 15-20 CM (6-8") LONG • A SLICE OF CARROT FOR THE FLAG
• I SMALL CARROT OR SPRING ONION FOR THE BOATMAN • I SMALL RED RADISH OR TOMATO
FOR THE BOATMAN'S HAT • I BAMBOO SKEWER • PINS • TOOTHPICKS

I

Cut a thin slice along the length
of the cucumber to give it a base.

Mark a line as shown in the diagram and cut along
the line, leaving one end attached, to create a flap.
Carefully bend the flap backwards and secure it
with a wooden skewer, piercing through the free
end of the flap and into the cucumber.

Scoop out the seeds and pulp and clean
the exposed cavity.

2

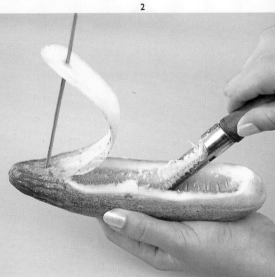

3

Make a zigzag border all around the rim
of the cavity.

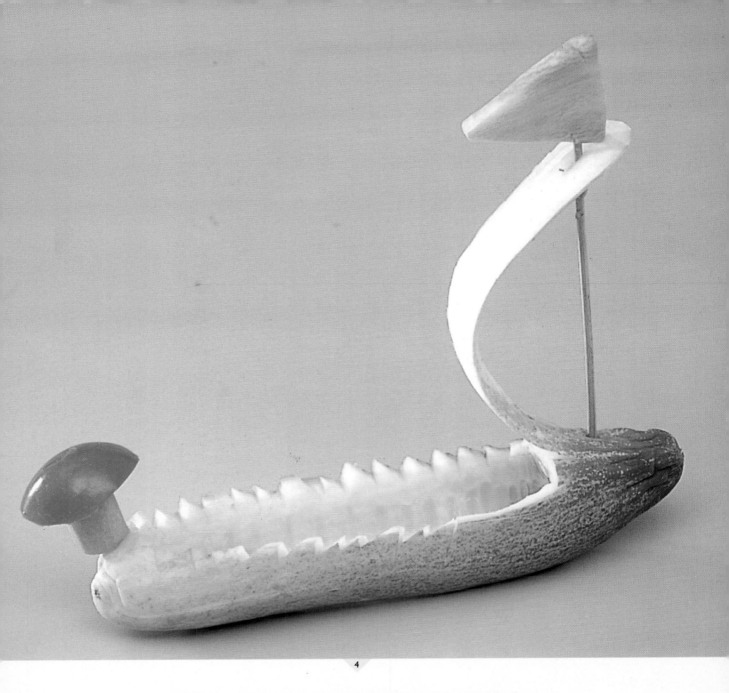

4

Shape the carrot slice into a triangular flag and attach it to the top of the skewer.
Cut a slice from the top of the red radish/tomato and fix it to a 5 cm (2") cylinder of carrot, or to the
bulb of a small spring onion, to make the boatman. Attach the boatman to the boat with a toothpick.

• I FAT CUCUMBER 15-20 CM (6-8") LONG
• I BIG CARROT OR RADISH • BAMBOO SKEWERS

C A R T

I

Cut off a slice from one end of the cucumber and discard.

From the same end cut two I cm (½") thick slices of cucumber for the wheels.

2

Stand the cucumber upright and remove a thin slice all down the length.

3

Parallel to this cut a strip I cm (½") wide and 5 cm (2") long. Cut again at right angles and discard this corner piece to expose the section that will form the handle.

4

Place the cucumber on the flat side; cut out and discard the seeds and pulp from within the handle.

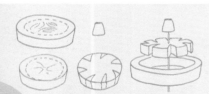

To make the wheels, cut out the seed portion from the centre of the two slices of cucumber and replace with a slice of carrot/radish cut to the same dimensions and thickness, after carving a pattern of spokes.

5

Stand the cart so that the handle is on top. Using a skewer, fix wheels in the middle of the cart body, on either side, resting the wheels on the tabletop. Allow the skewer to protrude beyond the wheels.

Pierce a piece of carrot or cucumber on the protruding skewer to make the hubcaps.

6

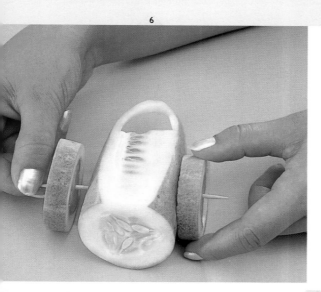

7

Thinly slice the carrot/radish and cut it to the same length as the body of the cart.

Mark a grid fence having 3 sections, then cut it out and remove the panels in between.

Insert a toothpick into each of the standing poles of the fence and fix them on the cart on the two long edges.

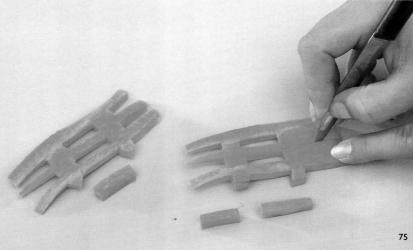

- 1 CUCUMBER, ABOUT 18 CM (7") LONG
- 1 LARGE GREEN CAPSICUM • TOOTHPICKS

COCONUT PALM

1

Cut off one end of the cucumber to form a base.

To fashion the trunk of the palm tree, make scalloped cuts in the skin of the cucumber, alternating the positions. Start at the bottom and work all round the vegetable to the top.

Immerse the cucumber in iced water for several hours to allow the cuts to open. (To reduce the soaking time, insert small pieces of any vegetable to keep the scallops open and discard them later.

2

For the palm fronds, cut the capsicum at the stem end, along the natural sections, making deep v-shapes on the lower edge. Discard the stem, the seeds and the fleshy centre.

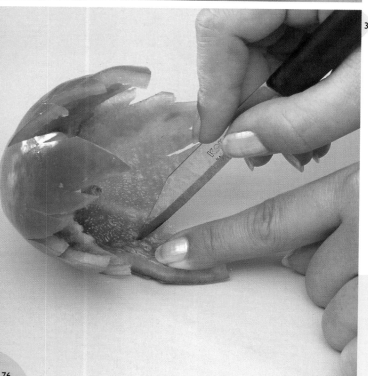

3

Cut zigzags in steps along the edge.

To assemble the palm, stand the cucumber trunk on its base and fix the capsicum over it with a toothpick through the centre.

SPRING IS EVERYWHERE
Birds, animals, trees and flowers, made from yams,
carrots cucumbers and turnips enliven the farmyard

THE BUFFET TABLE
Lilies, made from cucumbers,
set a cool, summer mood

- 1 MEDIUM-SIZED STRAIGHT CUCUMBER
- 1 STRAIGHT, THICK SPRING ONION BULB FOR THE CENTRE
- TOOTHPICK • RUBBER BAND

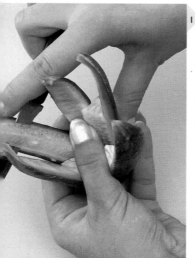

1

Starting from the top of the cucumber, cut out five evenly spaced petal shapes, stopping about 1 cm (½") from the bottom.

Gently separate these petals and remove the pulp from inside, leaving a smooth surface.

2

Within each petal, leaving a margin of almost 60 mm (¼"), cut out a smaller petal, which remains attached at the lower end.

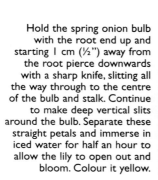

3

Push the smaller petal towards the centre.

Gather all five petals together and secure with a rubber band.

Invert the cucumber into a bowl of iced water with the outer petals spread outwards and leave for at least half an hour to let the flower bloom; drain.

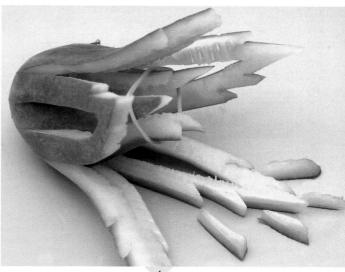

4

Hold one petal at a time and carve a zigzag border, making one straight cut and one slanting cut.

5

Hold the spring onion bulb with the root end up and starting 1 cm (½") away from the root pierce downwards with a sharp knife, slitting all the way through to the centre of the bulb and stalk. Continue to make deep vertical slits around the bulb. Separate these straight petals and immerse in iced water for half an hour to allow the lily to open out and bloom. Colour it yellow.

Release the inner petals of the cucumber lily from the rubber band. Pierce a skewer through the base of the cucumber lily and into the yellow onion lily to attach it to the centre.

• **4** BITTER GOURDS — A LONG ONE FOR THE TAIL FEATHERS, A SMALL ONE FOR THE WINGS, A CURVED ONE FOR THE HEAD AND A MEDIUM ONE FOR THE BODY • A BIG ROUND SLICE OF CARROT FOR THE BEAK • PEPPERCORNS FOR THE EYES • TOOTHPICKS   PINS

PARROT

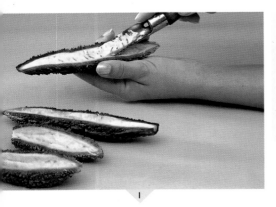

1

Cut the bitter gourds that are meant for the tail feathers and the wings into half lengthways and scoop out the seeds. You now have two hollow tail pieces and two hollow wing pieces.

2

For the tail feather, leave about 5 cm (2") from the stem end and cut strips all down the length. Cut the other tail feather in the same way.

3

For the wing, cut the stem end into a curve and cut strips all down the length. Cut the other wing in the same way.

4

Cut off 7.5 cm (3") from the curved bitter gourd that is meant for the head and scoop out the seeds to make it hollow.

5

Make two small cuts, about 2.5 cm (1") apart, along the cut edge.

6

Push the head on top of the fourth bitter gourd — the body of the bird. Fit and secure with pins.

Using pins, fix one tail feather at the end of the body so that the strips hang down.

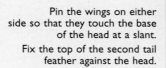

Pin the wings on either side so that they touch the base of the head at a slant.
Fix the top of the second tail feather against the head.

8

9

From a thick round slice of carrot, shape a curved beak.

10

Cut a rectangular slot in the inner curve of the head.

11

Insert the carrot beak into the head slot and fix with pins. Immerse the parrot in iced water for at least an hour so that the wings and tail take on a natural curve. Make small holes and insert the peppercorn eyes on either side of head.

CHRYSANTHEMUM

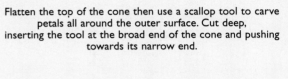

Shape the top of the turnip into a cone.

Flatten the top of the cone then use a scallop tool to carve petals all around the outer surface. Cut deep, inserting the tool at the broad end of the cone and pushing towards its narrow end.

2

3

Cut away a circular section from under the petals to fully expose them. Now carve a second row of petals to alternate with the first row and cut away a section to expose the petals.

Go on repeating the steps till the centre is reached. Trim the centre into a tip.

Immerse the chrysanthemum in iced water for half an hour.

Cut out chrysanthemum leaves from cabbage leaves. Attach the leaves to the flower with pins.

ROSE

Shape the top of the beetroot into a cone.

Flatten the top of the cone. With the tip of a knife, mark the outline of a series of 5-6 scallops around the base of the cone.

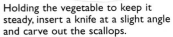

Holding the vegetable to keep it steady, insert a knife at a slight angle and carve out the scallops.

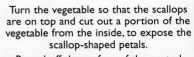

Trim the centre into a tip.

Immerse the flower in iced water for about an hour. Pierce a toothpick in the base of the flower.

NOTE: Turnips, potatoes or carrots may be used to make this rose.

Turn the vegetable so that the scallops are on top and cut out a portion of the vegetable from the inside, to expose the scallop-shaped petals.

Round off the surface of the central portion to make a cylindrical shape.

Cut out a second row of scallops on the cylinder, then cut away a portion of the vegetable to expose the petals, which should come in between the ones in the previous row.

Repeat the steps for the 3rd and 4th rows. Note that the petals will reduce in number and are positioned lower as you get closer to the centre.

1

Pare the beetroot and cut 4 or 5 thin slices for the petals and a small thick block to make a stopper.
Shape the carrot into a pointed cone.
Insert a toothpick into the stopper.

2

Stack the slices and make a cut from the centre to the outer edge.
Shape a slice into a shallow cone by overlapping the cut edges, as shown in the diagram. Insert the centre of the overlap onto the toothpick — this holds the cone in shape — and rest it against the stopper.

3

Shape another slice into a cone and attach it to the toothpick, as shown in the diagram, so that it comes inside the first and faces it.
Subsequent cones are made smaller by increasing their overlap. They are placed one inside the other and their points come in between the earlier pairs.

Fix the carrot cone on the protruding toothpick in the centre.
Immerse in iced water for at least an hour for it to bloom.
NOTE: A poppy can be made using slices of carrot, radish, potato or cucumber. To make the slices pliable, soak them in a solution of salt water for a few minutes.

4

GLADIOLI

1

Cut thin slices from a peeled beetroot.
Roll one slice tightly to resemble a gladioli bloom.

2

Leave about 2.5 cm (1") from the top of the drumstick and, working downwards, make deep cuts to create flaps, piercing almost to the middle of the drumstick. Stagger the positions of the flaps.

4

Cut a spring onion stem into 5 cm (2") pieces, slice it open and cut with scissors into pointed leaf-shapes.
Insert a leaf into the flaps in the drumstick along with some of the blooms.

3

Insert a bloom into the topmost flap in the drumstick. Secure it with a pin inserted at an angle from inside.

5

Continue inserting the blooms and leaves into the flaps till you have 8 or 10 blooms on the stalk.

6

To form large leaf sprays slit the tubes of broad spring onion greens through one side, open out and flatten.

Cut the greens with scissors into leaf shapes. Curl each leaf with the blade of the scissors. Fix on either side of the drumstick with pins.

NOTE: Gladioli blooms can be made out of turnip or carrot slices. To make the slices more pliable, soak them in a solution of salt water for a few minutes.

celebrations

90 Fruit Garnishes | 98 Festive Themes | 108 Children's Treats

• I LARGE APPLE • A PIECE OF CARROT FOR THE BEAK
• PEPPERCORNS OR MUSTARD SEEDS FOR THE EYES • TOOTHPICKS • PINS
• SOLUTION OF ½ LITRE WATER AND JUICE OF I LEMON

APPLE BIRD

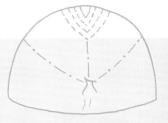

From the centre of the apple cut off a small, pointed, oval-shaped segment. Cut three more segments parallel to the first, so that you have four oval segments in all.

Slice off one-third of an apple just below the stem to give it a flat base. Reserve the cut-off section for the bird's head and neck.

From the centre of the reserved one-third of the apple cut a I cm (½") wide slice which includes the peel.

Cut the straight side of the slice into a curve to shape the neck and insert toothpicks at both ends. Cut a triangle from the carrot to make a beak.

Cut similar sets of segments from both sides of the apple after finding the centre of each side. Note that the segments from each of the 3 cuts should be kept together.

Spray the exposed apple and the segments with the solution of water and lemon juice to prevent discolouration.

Arrange each set of ovals in the space from which they were cut, staggering them so that they emerge one out of the other.

To keep them in place pierce a toothpick or pin through the third wedge into the apple body, then place the smallest wedge over it.

Attach the beak to the head and pierce the opposite end of the slice into the body of the bird.

Make small holes and insert the peppercorn or mustard seed eyes on either side of the head. After the bird is complete, spray it with the solution of lemon and water to prevent discolouration.

PROUD AS A PEACOCK
The peacock, made from watermelon
gets a round of applause

• I LARGE, GREEN WATERMELON • I SMALL CARROT FOR THE BEAK
• I PAPAYA OR MARSH MELON • 200 G GREEN SEEDLESS GRAPES • 200 G BLACK GRAPES
(OR ANY OTHER FRUIT OF YOUR CHOICE) • 13-15 LONG SKEWERS • TOOTHPICKS • PINS

WATERMELON PEACOCK

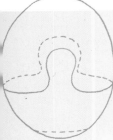

Cut a slice from the stem side of the watermelon to make a flat base.

Place the watermelon on its base and mark off the shape, in which the smaller curve is the head of the peacock and the larger curve, shown by the dotted line, is the tail portion.

Cut around the head and tail outline, removing excess pieces of watermelon and keeping them aside. Cut out excess fruit from the centre of the watermelon and level it out.

Decorate the rim with a zigzag design.

For the wings, take a piece of leftover watermelon and slice out the red pulp neatly.

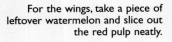

Cut out 2 mango-shaped wings.

Make a crown with a smaller piece of watermelon rind, cutting the base into a curve to fit the head.

Carve deep zigzags on the crown and along the sides of the wings.

5

Cut out curving grooves on the neck of the bird as in the picture.

Pin the wings firmly on either side of the bird with 2 or 3 toothpicks or pins.

Cut out a tiny circle on the head for the eye and insert a peppercorn in the centre.

6

Carve a pointed beak from the carrot.

Slit it lengthways through the centre so that it looks partly open.

7

Pin the beak to the head with a toothpick. Attach the crown to the head with two toothpicks.

Using a melon scoop, scoop out small balls from the papaya and from the remaining watermelon, keeping them separate.

Place the green and black grapes in separate piles.

Cut out small green triangles from the melon rind. Skewer the fruit in the same order for each skewer, ending with the triangle of rind. Using a spare skewer, make 13 holes at regular intervals on the tail of the bird. Insert the skewers into the holes. Pile up the centre of the bird with the remaining fruit.

• I MEDIUM, ROUND GREEN WATERMELON

WATERMELON ROSE

1

Cut one end of the watermelon wide enough to form a base.

Mark the outline of equidistant sepals all around to form the calyx, going almost halfway up; deepen the outlines.

2

Between the sepals of the calyx make semi-circular incisions; remove the green rind below the incision to create a row of white petals.

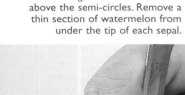

3

Remove segments of watermelon above the semi-circles. Remove a thin section of watermelon from under the tip of each sepal.

4

Carve the next row of semi-circular incisions. These and subsequent rows of petals will be the pink or red of the watermelon.

5

Continue in the same way till you reach the top. The shape gets gradually narrower. Make sure you do not scoop so deep that the seeds are visible.

Cut the centre into a pyramid shape and remove it to leave a hollow.

6

Carve zigzag edges on the calyx and mark the veins.

ENTERTAIN WITH A FLAIR
This delightful fruit platter will impress every time

SWEET LIME FLOWER

1

Mark the outline of six petals on the skin of the fruit so that it is equally divided into six part. Pierce the outline carefully, going only skin deep.

Gently open out the petals, peeling the skin almost to the bottom and preserving the fruit in the centre.

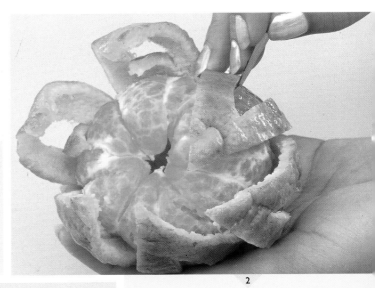

2

Cut a smaller, inner petal inside each segment, leaving it attached at the base, and push it out.

• 1 MEDIUM-SIZED CARROT • 1 MEDIUM-SIZED CUCUMBER

1

Cut a curved, elongated portion of the carrot from one side and discard.
Similarly, cut a portion from the other side and discard. The middle portion is used to carve the leaf.

2

Pare the carrot piece so that it forms a leaf shape, pointed at one end, with the leaf-stem at the other end.

3

Engrave the central vein as a continuation of the stem.

4

Cut a wedge-shaped design along the edge of the leaf.
To emphasise the central vein, scoop out deep grooves from either side; then make curving branch veins.

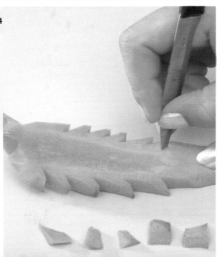

5

Pare away the extra thickness under the leaf to accentuate its curve. Immerse the leaf in iced water.

For cucumber leaves, cut the cucumber in half lengthways and use its rind and natural curves as the leaf surface.
Variation: Instead of marking the leaf-veins with grooves, make slits which go all the way through the leaf.

- 1 YAM OR ASH PUMPKIN (*PETHA*)
- 1 CARROT FOR THE ANTLERS AND TAIL • 2 PEPPERCORNS FOR THE EYES
- 1 RED CHERRY FOR THE NOSE • TOOTHPICKS

REINDEER

Make a paper pattern in the shape of a reindeer.

Cut a regular, straight-sided block out of the yam/ash pumpkin. It should be about 60 mm (¼") thick.

Trace the outline of the reindeer on the block. Hold the knife perpendicular and pierce slowly along the edge of the pattern to avoid the under section getting mutilated

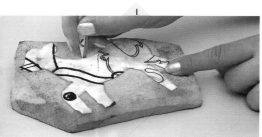

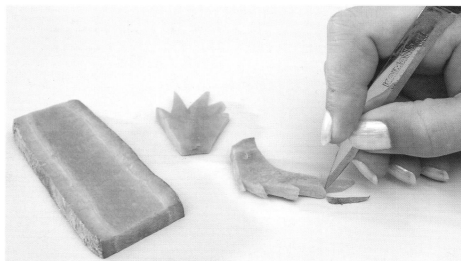

Cut a long slice of carrot and carve out the antlers and tail.

Make small holes and insert the peppercorn eyes and a small red cherry for the nose.

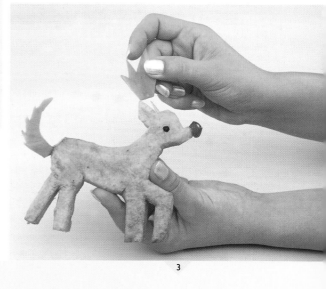

Fix the antlers and tail on the reindeer with toothpicks or pins.

• I ASH PUMPKIN (*PETHA*) • TOOTHPICKS

Make a paper pattern of a sleigh. Cut thin slices down the length of the ash pumpkin on both sides to create a flat block. Cut two rectangular slices, each about 4 cm (1½") thick.

Place the paper pattern on one slice and trace the outline of the sleigh.

Hold the knife perpendicular and pierce slowly along the edge of the pattern to avoid the under section getting mutilated.

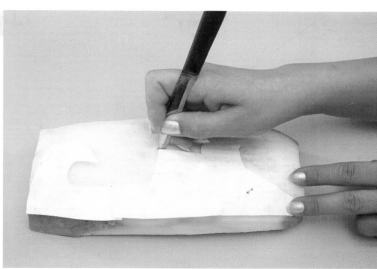

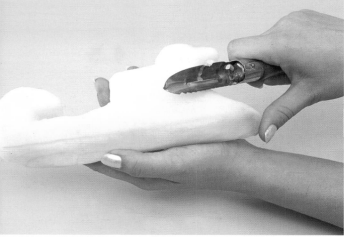

With a peeler, refine the shape. Repeat with the second slice.

Place the two pieces of the sleigh side by side. The front ends of the sleigh should be closer to each other than the rear ends. Cut a rectangular block from the pumpkin and, with toothpicks, fit it between the two sleigh pieces at the rear. With a toothpick fit a reindeer in the front.

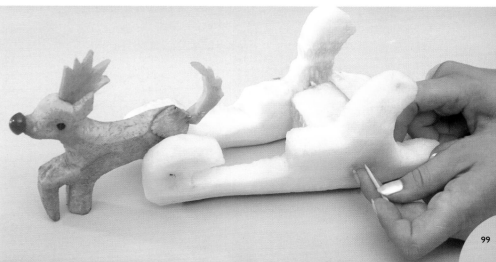

99

X'MAS CHEER
It's fun time with
Mr. Snowman, made from turnips

JINGLE BELLS
Here comes Santa, made from apples
with his Reindeer, made from pumpkin

• I MEDIUM-SIZED RED APPLE • I LARGE RED APPLE • I SMALL RED APPLE • I FAT RED RADISH • I BIG SLICE OF BRINJAL (AUBERGINE) • A PIECE OF WHITE RADISH • PEPPERCORNS • A PIECE OF CARROT • I OBLONG SPRING ONION BULB • 2 SMALL GHERKINS (*TENDLIS*) OR OTHER VEGETABLE FOR THE SHOES • SKEWERS • PINS • TOOTHPICKS • LEMON JUICE

I

Fix the medium-sized apple on the large apple with a skewer.

Slice off a section from one side of the medium-sized apple to make an oval face.

Rub the exposed white section of apple with lemon juice to prevent discolouration. Make small holes and
insert the peppercorn eyes and a sliver of red apple for the mouth.

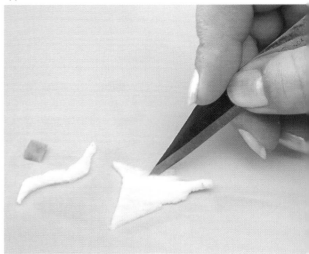

2

Cut a small carrot triangle for the nose. From a slice of white radish cut out a moustache and a beard shape.

Make a cap by cutting off the stem end of the red radish, but retaining the root. Fix a small white ball, carved from the white radish, to the end of the root. Cut a strip of white radish 60 mm (¼") wide, wrap it around the base of the cap and fix it with a pin.

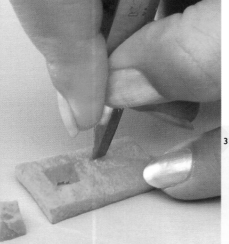

3

From a slice of carrot cut out a rectangle and carve it to resemble a buckle.

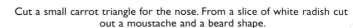

Attach the cap to the head with a toothpick.

From a 60 mm (¼") thick slice of brinjal pare the skin to make a belt.

Attach the belt and buckle using pins.

Cut the ends off the gherkins and fix them below the body for Santa's shoes, or cut out shoe shapes from watermelon rind or other vegetable.

5

Cut the third apple into half and cut 2 thick slices from one half.

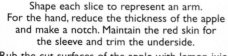

6

Shape each slice to represent an arm. For the hand, reduce the thickness of the apple and make a notch. Maintain the red skin for the sleeve and trim the underside.

Rub the cut surfaces of the apple with lemon juice to prevent discolouration.

7

Trim an oblong spring onion bulb at the stem and pin it across one shoulder as a sack.

Attach the arms at the shoulders to the apple body, positioning one arm over the sack and the other hanging down.

103

- 1 SMALL TURNIP FOR THE HEAD • 1 SLIGHTLY LARGER TURNIP FOR THE BODY • A SLICE FROM THE TOP OF A BRINJAL (AUBERGINE) FOR THE HAT • 1 CARROT FOR THE NECK, HANDS, NOSE, SCARF AND BROOM • PEPPERCORNS FOR THE EYES • BAMBOO SKEWERS • TOOTHPICKS • PINS

SNOWMAN

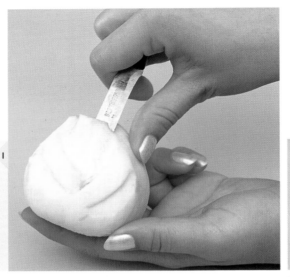

Peel the turnips then cut thin slices to flatten the top and bottom. Outline the arms on the bigger turnip then deepen the outline into a groove.

Carve the arms by removing the turnip along the incision and cutting away a portion of the chest to reduce the curve.

Attach the two turnips together with a skewer after inserting a small cylinder of carrot for the neck.

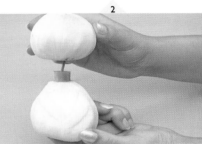

Hollow out the underside of the slice of brinjal to fit on the head and attach with a toothpick.

From thin slices of carrot cut out the hands, the scarf and the broom.

Make small holes and insert the peppercorn eyes and a semicircular wedge of carrot or red radish for the mouth. Attach a triangular piece of carrot for the nose, using a pin.

Fix the hands to the arms using small bit of toothpick. Wrap the scarf around the neck. Place the broom against the body and fix it between the hands.

Cut a large slice from the stem end of the small watermelon/ papaya to make a flat base.
Remove all the pulp from the inside of the fruit, leaving a shell about 2.5 cm (1") thick. If a watermelon is used save a thin layer of red pulp on the inside.

Stand the shell on its base and mark a circle on the top, about 7.5 cm (3") in diameter. Score the outline.

Below this carve out inverted equilateral triangles which touch the circle, about 1 cm (½") apart. Cut right through the rind to expose the inside.

1

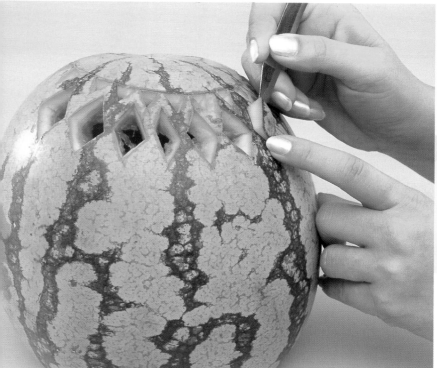

2

Cut successive rows of diamond shapes, positioning each row in between the previous one.

3

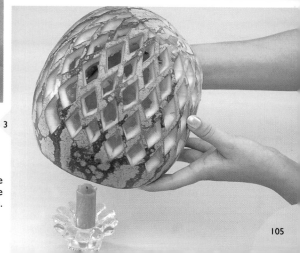

Continue with the pattern till 10 cm (4") from the base. Place the carved lamp over a candle. Decorate with flowers of your choice.

105

FESTIVAL OF LIGHTS
A beautiful Diwali lamp, made from watermelon,
for this festive day

- A BLOCK OF YAM OR ASH PUMPKIN (*PETHA*) FOR THE WALL • I LARGE, ROUND BRINJAL (AUBERGINE) • I LIME
- 4 THIN, LONG CARROTS • I SMALL BRINJAL (AUBERGINE) • 2 SMALL GHERKINS (*TENDLIS*) OR OTHER VEGETABLE
FOR THE SHOES • A PIECE OF RED RADISH/CARROT • SKEWERS • TOOTHPICKS • FELT PEN • BRUSH • FOOD COLOUR

HUMPTY DUMPTY

1

Make a wall by shaping a block out of the yam/ash pumpkin. Make the top flat. Do not remove the rind, if any.

Use food colour to paint a wall design on the front surface, or, cut narrow horizontal bars, and then individual vertical ones, alternating their positions to look like a brick or stone wall.

2

Cut off a slice from the bottom of the brinjal, saving the slice for the hat brim. Remove the stem from the top, but retain the calyx to act as a collar.

Insert a skewer in the wall and set the brinjal on it.

3

Paint a face on the lime and insert a sliver of carrot or red radish for the mouth.

4

For the hat, use the brinjal slice for the rim; cut off the stem end of the small brinjal and fix it as the crown. Attach the hat to the head with a toothpick or pin.

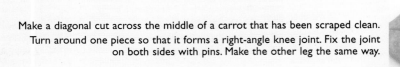

5

Make a diagonal cut across the middle of a carrot that has been scraped clean. Turn around one piece so that it forms a right-angle knee joint. Fix the joint on both sides with pins. Make the other leg the same way.

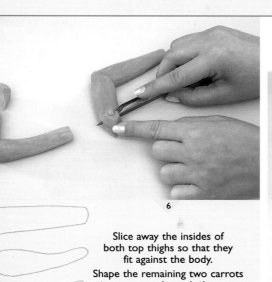

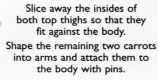

6

Slice away the insides of both top thighs so that they fit against the body.

Shape the remaining two carrots into arms and attach them to the body with pins.

7

Pierce a skewer in the middle of the brinjal and fix the head, against the calyx collar.

Attach the legs to the body with pins.

Make two shoes by cutting out a rectangular slot in each gherkin and inserting the ends of the legs. Use pins if required.

CHILDREN'S TREATS

• 1 SMALL LEMON, FOR THE HEAD • THE FIBRE FROM 2 CORNCOBS, FOR THE HAIR • 1 LARGE RADISH
FOR THE BODY AND THE NECK • 1 CARROT FOR THE SASH, BUTTONS, HANDS AND HAT
• 2-3 CABBAGE LEAVES FOR THE SKIRT • 1 SMALL TURNIP FOR THE COLLAR • TOOTHPICKS • PINS • FELT PEN

S N O W   W H I T E   A N D   T H E   S E V E N   D W A R F S

S N O W   W H I T E

1

Remove the outer sheaths of the corn cobs, take a firm hold of the silken fibre (hair) on the tip and gently pull it off the cob (see p. 118, *Corn Doll*). Lay it on a flat surface.

Similarly, pull out the hair from the second corncob. (The cobs are not required).

Place all the hair on one end of a strip of adhesive tape and turn the tape over to form a hair switch.

2

Place the hair switch on the lemon and secure with pins.

4

Twist the hair into a bun or make any other hairstyle and secure with pins.

NOTE: Instead of rolling the hair into a bun, it may be left hanging down, or made into the hairstyle of your choice.

3

Turn the shorter length of hair to make a padding, then turn the longer hair over it, giving it a slight lift.

Gather all the hair and fix it with a bit of tape to keep it in place.

5

Cut a 12 cm (5") section from the radish, 4-5 cm (1½"-2") in diameter.

Almost halfway down the radish cut away a portion like a triangle from either side to make a waist. Shape the part above the waist into a shallow cone.

Use a peeler to round out the upper and lower parts of the body. Carve long, wedge-shaped cuts on the skirt front to resemble folds.

Mark out the arms/sleeves with shallow grooves. Carve away some of the radish between and around the sleeves so that they are raised.

7

Pass a toothpick through a cylindrical piece of radish for the neck and fix one end on the body; pierce the other end of the toothpick into the lemon head.

Draw the eyes, nose and mouth on the lemon, using a felt pen.

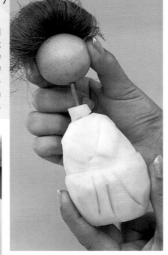

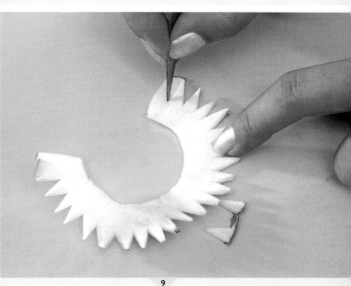

8

Cut and shape a thick slice of carrot into a hat, scooping out a hollow underneath so that it fits on the head.

Attach the hat to the head with pins.

9

Shape the top of the turnip into a cone, then cut a curving slice to make a collar. Scallop the edge of the collar.

Fix the collar around the neck with pins.

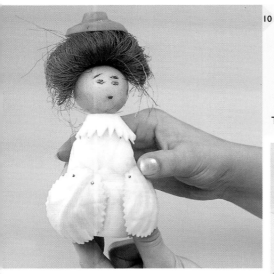

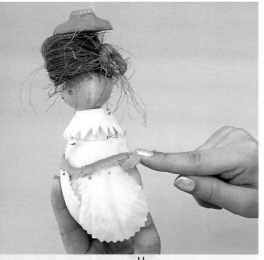

Cut a long thin strip of carrot for the sash and tie it at the back into a bow. Attach with a pin. Use small round carrot slices for buttons and fix them on the body. Shape hands out of pieces of carrot and attach them to the sleeve ends with a sliver of toothpick. Add accessories of your choice, such as earrings and a basket.

Trim two cabbage leaves and fix them at the waist on either side with pins.

Make a basket out of the small red radish. Mark as shown in diagram and remove the shaded portion.

Remove the pulp to make a handle (see Vendor p. 122).

Two hair styles for Snow White

• RED RADISHES OF DIFFERENT SIZES, SOME LONG AND SOME ROUND • A PIECE OF WHITE RADISH FOR THE BEARD • 2 SMALL GHERKINS (*TENDLIS*) OR OTHER VEGETABLE FOR THE SHOES • A PIECES OF BRINJAL (AUBERGINE) FOR THE BELT • A PIECE OF CARROT FOR THE NOSE • PINS • TOOTHPICKS

DWARF

1

Select two red radishes of different sizes and cut the base of the smaller one.
Cut the base and the top of the larger one (see diagram).
Slice off a round section from one side of the small red radish to expose the white surface underneath for the face.
Fix the small red radish onto the larger one with a toothpick.

2

Make a beard out of the white radish.

3

Cut a long red radish lengthways into quarters and use two of the pieces for arms.
Shape the ends of the arms into hands by reducing the thickness.

4

Fix the arms to the body at the shoulders using pins.
Make small holes and insert the peppercorn eyes. Attach the beard with pins.

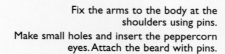

5

Attach a triangular carrot nose and a red radish mouth using slivers of toothpicks or pins.
Pare the skin off the brinjal and cut a long strip.
Fix the strip of brinjal around the middle of the body as a belt.
Vary the appearances of the seven dwarfs by making different styles of beard and by changing the shapes and angles used in the body pieces.

SNOW WHITE AND THE SEVEN DWARFS

Cut a thick section from the cucumber and shape it roughly into a square.

Place the square block of cucumber with the flat side down and cut it in half diagonally.

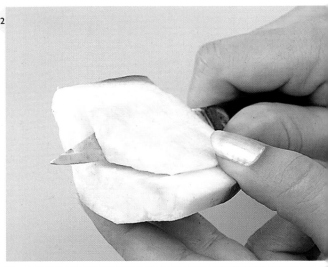

Shape one of these halves into a roof with two sloping sides by removing the inner seed portion.

Cut out a thick slice from the middle of the carrot.

Place the carrot piece on a flat surface and cut it to resemble the front of a cottage.

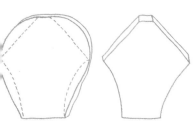

Attach the cucumber roof on top of the cottage with pins.

Cut a window and a door from a piece of cucumber rind and attach them to the front of the cottage with pins.

For the chimney, cut a rectangular piece of carrot about 3-4 cm (1" x 1½"). Cut the bottom at a slant to match the angle of the roof.

Carve out a square rim on the top of the chimney, or, attach a square piece of seedless cucumber to create the rim.

5

6

Mount the house on a base such as a small melon or pumpkin, or on a rectangular block of cucumber.

Place a bar made out of carrot across the door and attach the chimney with a toothpick to the side of the roof.

• 2 CORNCOBS FOR THE HAIR AND THE BODY • 1 SMALL LEMON • 2 RED CHILLIES • 2 SMALL GHERKINS (*TENDLIS*), PUMPKIN RIND, OR OTHER VEGETABLE • 1 COCKTAIL UMBRELLA • 1 LARGE PIECE OF PUMPKIN, • 1 MEDIUM CARROT FOR THE STOLE • ADHESIVE TAPE • SCISSORS • HAMMER • PINS • TOOTHPICKS • FELT PEN

CORN DOLL

1 Remove and discard the outer soiled sheaths on one of the corncobs.

Pull some of the leaves away from the corncob.

Take a firm hold of the silken fibre (hair) on the tip and gently pull it off the cob. Lay it on a flat surface.

Similarly, pull out the hair from the second corncob. (The rest of this cob is not required).

2

Place all the hair on one end of a strip of adhesive tape and turn the tape over to form a hair switch.

3

Place the hair switch on the lemon and secure with pins.

4

Turn the shorter length of hair to make a padding, then turn the longer hair over it, giving it a slight lift.

Gather all the hair and fix it with a bit of tape to keep it in place.

Twist the hair into a bun or make any other hairstyle and secure with pins.

5

Cut almost half the cob from the top end.
Trim the leaves at different lengths to make an attractive ruffled skirt.

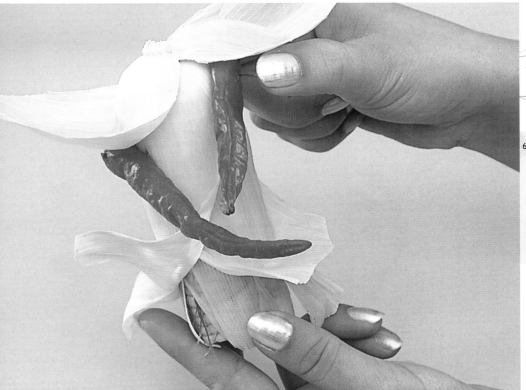

6

Pin the two red chillies as arms under the topmost leaf on either side.

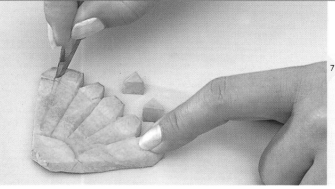

Cut a triangular slice of pumpkin for the fan
then shape the top into a curve and the bottom into a point.

Mark a small curve above the pointed end, then mark 3 or 4 long, radiating lines towards the edge, deepening them for emphasis.

Cut out scallops along the curved edge to
resemble a fan.

8

Place the fan in the middle of the body, wrap the
chilli arms over it and fix with pins.

Insert a skewer into the bottom of the corncob,
using a hammer if required. Make a 5 cm (2") base
from part of the pumpkin.

Insert the skewer into the pumpkin to attach the
doll to the base.

9

Insert a skewer into the top of the corncob, using a hammer if required.
Attach the lemon head onto the skewer.

Draw the eyes, nose and mouth on the lemon with a felt pen. Cut out loops of carrot for earrings and fix on either side of the head with pins.

Cut a thin long slice of carrot for the stole and pin it around the neck of the corn doll.

Decorate the base with leaves or flowers.

• 2 OBLONG BRINJALS (AUBERGINES) OF EQUAL SIZE • 1 LONGER BRINJAL • 1 LEMON • A PIECE OF BRINJAL OR CARROT • A PIECE OF WHITE RADISH • 2 GHERKINS (*TENDLIS*) OR OTHER VEGETABLE FOR THE SHOES • 2 RED RADISHES OR GREEN TOMATOES • SOME HERBS • 2 FRESH RED CHILLIES • TOOTHPICKS • BAMBOO SKEWER • FELT PENS

1

Cut off the stems of the small brinjals, along with the calyx.

Carve out a vertical curved section from one, starting near the top and ending well before the bottom, as shown in the diagram.

2

Fit the second small brinjal into this cavity and attach the two with toothpicks.

Level the tops of the pataloons and level the bottoms as well, so that they can stand.

Insert toothpicks on the top of the pantaloons and pierce them into the base of the long brinjal, the body.

Shorten the stem of the long brinjal, leaving a small section to serve as the neck.

3

4

Fix the lemon on to the neck with a toothpick.

Shape a hat from the top of a small brinjal, hollow out the underside and attach it to the head with a toothpick.

Draw slanting eyes, a nose and mouth with felt pens.

Cut a beard out of a thin slice of radish.
Attach the curved side of the beard under the mouth.

5

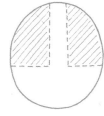

Make baskets out of the red radishes.
Mark as shown in the diagram and remove the shaded portion.
Remove the pulp to make a handle.

6

Pierce the skewer through the shoulders and thread a chilli through each end for arms.
Cut one end off the gherkins and fix them to the base of the pantaloons as shoes.
Hang the baskets laden with herbs or flowers from the arms.

7

• 3 FAT CARROTS • 3 SMALL LEMONS • ANY SMALL ROUND VEGETABLE (BRINJAL, TURNIP, RED RADISH) FOR THE HATS • SPRING ONION GREENS OR A STRIP OF CARROT FOR THE WAISTBANDS • RADISH, LADY FINGER AND GHERKIN FOR THE MUSICAL INSTRUMENTS • TOOTHPICKS • PINS • FELT PENS

MUSICIANS

Cut the narrow end of the carrot into a cone shape.

Almost halfway down the carrot cut away a portion like a triangle from either side to make a waist and shape the body.

At the waist make a deep groove where the waistband will come.

Round off the body with a peeler.

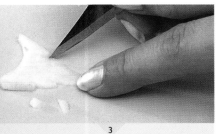

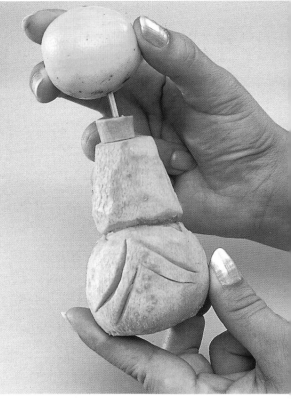

3

Cut out a beard from a slice of radish.

Paint the eyes and mouth on the lemon with a felt pen. Attach the beard with pins. For the hat, cut a segment from the top of a turnip, hollow it out and fit it on the lemon head, using pins.

Wrap a spring onion leaf or a strip of carrot around the body as a waistband and fix it with a pin.

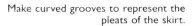

Make curved grooves to represent the pleats of the skirt.

Using a toothpick, fix a small 1 cm (½") thick slice of carrot for the neck and attach a lemon for the head.

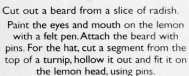

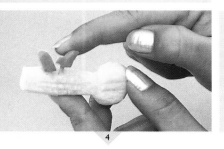

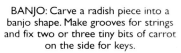

4

BANJO: Carve a radish piece into a banjo shape. Make grooves for strings and fix two or three tiny bits of carrot on the side for keys.

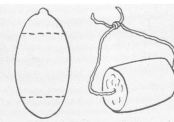

5

DHOL (drum): Use a gherkin (*tendli*), or a piece of any suitable vegetable for the drum. Cut off the two ends of the gherkin to get a drum shape. With a needle, draw a string through the drum, tie a knot to form a loop.

6

TRUMPET: Use a curved lady finger, green chilli or carrot for the trumpet. Pierce a toothpick through the trumpet.

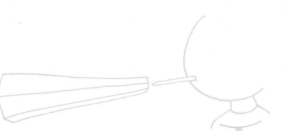

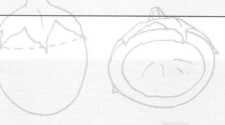

7

Cut tapered pieces of carrot lengthways into half to make arms and round off the broad ends of each with a peeler to make shoulders. For the hands, reduce the thickness of the arm and make a notch.

8

Vary the character of the three musicians by changing the body shape, height, hat and dress style. Carve grooves on one of the hats to resemble turban folds.

BANJO PLAYER: Lay the instrument against the body of the banjo player and position his arms and hands on the instrument.

DHOL (drum) PLAYER: Hang the drum over the neck of the drum player. Position his hands against the drum and fix them with pins.

TRUMPETER: Attach the narrow end of the trumpet against the mouth of the trumpeter. Position his hands on the instrument and fix them with pins on either side.

PAGODA

• I LONG, FAT CARROT

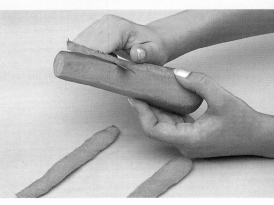

1

Cut off a slice from the broad end of the carrot and 2.5 cm (1")
or so from the narrow end.

On the flat broad end mark the outline of a pentagon of 5 equal
sides and slice along these markings, all the way down, to make
the whole block pentagonal,
following roughly the natural slant of the carrot.

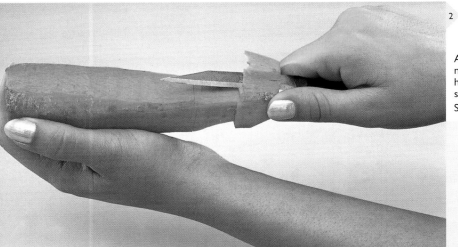

2

About 2.5 cm (1") below the
narrow end, the top of the pagoda, make a deep
horizontal groove all around and carve away a
section of the carrot below this to get a ledge.

Shape the top section into a pointed cone.

3

Make another deep groove parallel to the first, 2.5 cm (1")
below the cone. Remove the carrot above the cut to form a
panel on each side. This will make the top storey of the pagoda.

Make another groove 1 cm (½") below the previous one and
parallel to it. This will make the roof of the next storey.

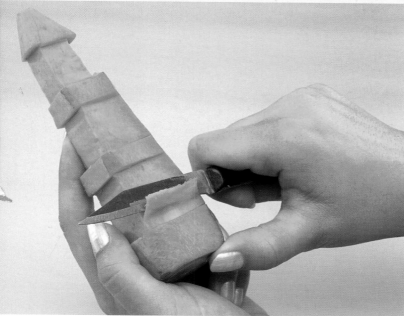

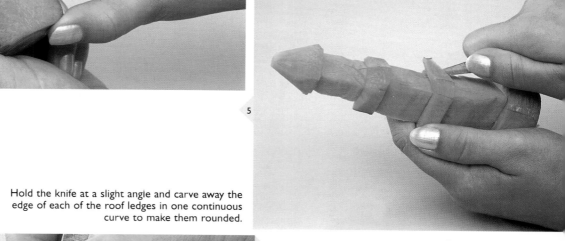

Repeat the steps ending with a high platform, the base of the pagoda.

5

Hold the knife at a slight angle and carve away the edge of each of the roof ledges in one continuous curve to make them rounded.

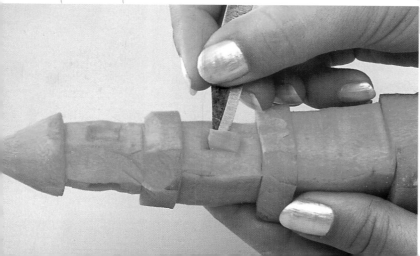

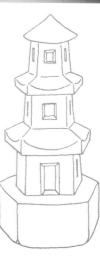

6

Carve out a small square window on each of the walls and a door on one of the ground-floor walls.

127

A PAGODA IN CHINATOWN